PRECIS

**A workbook for
students of librarianship**

PRECIS

A workbook for
students of librarianship

Michael J. Ramsden
M.Soc.Sc., B.A., F.L.A., A.L.A.A.
Head, Department of Librarianship
Royal Melbourne Institute of Technology

CLIVE BINGLEY LONDON

First published 1981 by Clive Bingley Ltd,
16 Pembridge Road, London W11.
Copyright © 1981 Michael J. Ramsden.
All rights reserved.
Set in 10 on 12 point Press Roman by Allset.
Printed and bound in the UK by
Redwood Burn Ltd of Trowbridge and Esher.

British Library Cataloguing in Publication Data

Ramsden, Michael John
    PRECIS. — (Outlines of modern librarianship).
    1. PRECIS (Indexing system) — Programmed
    instruction
    I. Title   II. Series
    029.5   Z695.92

    ISBN 0-85157-334-7

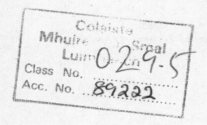

CONTENTS

Preface   7
Definitions   9
Reference sheet: Role operators   10
Introduction   13

Part I: SYNTAX

Unit 1
PRECIS entry format   22
Production of entries   23
Filing   25
Conventions   25

Unit 2
Differences   31

Unit 3
Main line operators 0-3   42

Unit 4
Interposed operators p, q and r   52

Unit 5
Main line operators 4 and 6   62
Some indexing problems   65

Unit 6
Coding of locality names   68

Unit 7
Concept interlinks: Operators s and t   74

Unit 8
Coordinate concepts   83
Theme interlinks   84

5

Two-way interactions   86
Directional properties   86
Compound agent   88

Part II: THE SEMANTIC PART OF PRECIS

Unit 9
References   92

Unit 10
Coding of references   98

Part III: MANIPULATION CODES

Unit 11
Computer manipulation codes   106

Part IV: PRESENT AND FUTURE

Unit 12
Applications   112
Examples of foreign language entries   113

MODEL ANSWERS

Checking exercise 1   120
Checking exercise 2   123
Checking exercise 3   127
Checking exercise 4   130
Checking exercise 5   133
Checking exercise 6   136
Checking exercise 7   139
Checking exercise 8   142
Checking exercise 9   145
Checking exercise 10   146
Checking exercise 11   148
Checking exercise 12   149

PREFACE

This workbook has been designed as a self-instructional package to teach the elements of the relatively new system of alphabetical subject indexing which is called PRECIS. It is divided into an introduction, explaining the reason for the development of the system, followed by twelve units, each unit being accompanied by a checking exercise which covers the material dealt with in the unit as well as reinforcing material from earlier units. Model answers for these checking exercises appear at the end of the workbook and the user should work through the checking exercises and compare his (or her) answers with the model answers before proceeding to the next unit. It is suggested that a score of less than seven correct strings for the string-writing questions, or more than two errors in the questions requiring entries to be written for given strings, indicates a need to re-read the unit before proceeding to the next.

This workbook has been developed over years of teaching PRECIS at the Royal Melbourne Institute of Technology. It was based initially on material supplied by the National Library of Australia, and I wish to acknowledge a very great debt of gratitude to the staff of the National Library. Without their help in supplying examples and exercise material we could not have begun to teach PRECIS in 1974 and this workbook could not have been developed. I am also grateful to Derek Austin for his interest and encouragement and for his always helpful comments. I have been assisted in developing the workbook by the comments of the students who have used it over the years, and that help too I gratefully acknowledge. The work has now reached a stage of development at which it is offered to a wider audience in the belief that it may be of some general use to teachers, to students and to librarians who may wish to know more about a system which post-dates their formal professional education.

Michael J Ramsden
May 1980

DEFINITIONS

1.1 Role operator: A code symbol which indicates the grammatical role or function of the term which follows it, and which regulates the order of terms in a string.

1.2 String: An ordered sequence of terms preceded by role operators. (Also referred to as a "concept string").

1.3 Concept: Usually defined as a single idea or unit of thought. However in PRECIS the definition is more precise. A concept is a unit of thought which, being expressed in words selected from natural language, can logically be matched by one of the role operators. For example, "Pest control" consists of two concepts because it may be analysed into two terms each of which can be introduced by its own role operator:
  (1) pests
  (2) control

1.4 Term: The verbal representation of a concept which may consist of one or more words, eg PRIME MINISTER.

2 There are three parts to PRECIS:

2.1 The syntax which is embodied in the system of role operators.

2.2 The semantic part which is embodied in the procedure for generating references to reflect *a priori* relationships.

2.3 The manipulation codes which instruct the computer to produce entries from a string.

REFERENCE SHEET

Role operators

MAIN LINE OPERATORS.
Every string must begin with one
of 0-2

Environment of observed system	0	Location
Observed system: Core operators	1	key system: object of transitive action; agent of intransitive action.
	2	Action/Effect
	3	Agent of transitive action; Aspects; Factors

Change of typography introduced
by remaining main line operators:
4-6 print in italics in display and
implement inverted pattern when
in lead.

Data relating to observer	4	Viewpoint-as-form
Selected instance	5	Sample population/Study region
Presentation of data	6	Target/Form

INTERPOSED OPERATORS.
May be inserted between main
line operators

Dependent elements	p	Part/Property
	q	Member of quasi-generic group
	r	Aggregate
Concept interlinks	s	Role definer
	t	Author attributed association
Coordinate concept	g	Coordinate concept

10

DIFFERENCING OPERATORS.
Have semantic function—
introduce adjectives qualifying
or focusing other terms.
Prefixed by $

h Non-lead direct difference
i Lead direct difference
k Non-lead indirect difference
m Lead indirect difference
n Non-lead parenthetical difference
o Lead parenthetical difference
d Date as difference

CONNECTIVES. Components
of linking phrases. Prefixed by $

v Downwards reading component
w Upwards reading component

THEME INTERLINKS

x First element in coordinate theme
y Subsequent element in coordinate theme
z Element of common theme

INTRODUCTION

1 PRECIS is an acronym which stands for Preserved Context Indexing System. The system was developed at the British National Bibliography during 1969 and 1970 as a part of the UK MARC Project, a project to develop a system for producing machine-readable bibliographic records.

2 One of the early objects of the UK MARC Project was to establish whether bibliographic data held in machine-readable form, and organised to a standard format for international exchange purposes, could also be used as the source for entries in the national bibliography. The conclusion that this was in fact feasible became the starting point for PRECIS.

3 The *British national bibliography* is a classified catalogue, ie, standard catalogue entries are arranged under classification symbols in the main sequence of the bibliography. Before we go any further we should consider the structure of the classified catalogue since an understanding of that structure is essential for an understanding of the original purpose of PRECIS.

4 *The classified catalogue*

4.1 In a classified catalogue the main sequence of entries is filed in subject order, according to the symbols of a classification scheme. In the case of the *British national bibliography*, as also in the *Australian national bibliography*, the classification scheme is the Dewey Decimal Classification. Thus in BNB and ANB the entries for documents on Australian history all appear at 994, since that is the Dewey number for this subject. Similarly documents on cricket appear at 796.358.

4.2 Users will, of course, express their subject requirements in words, for example "cricket", "Australian history" or "The effects of ionising

13

radiation on man". There is thus a need for some means by which a user may ascertain what is the code symbol for the subject on which he or she requires information.

4.3 A classified catalogue thus requires a *subject index*, ie, an index which "translates" subjects expressed in words ("natural language") into the appropriate classification numbers, eg, Cricket : 796.358. The subject index functions very much like the index to a book except that, instead of referring to page numbers, it refers to classification numbers. An extract from the subject index to an issue of the *British national bibliography* appears below.

Figure 1
Subject index

Landforms	551.4
Landowners. England	
Agreements with local authorities: Agreements on	
landscape conservation — *Reports, surveys*	719'.0942
Landrover cars	
to 1978	629.22'22
Landscape conservation. England	
Agreements between landowners & local authorities —	
Reports, surveys	719'.0942
Organisations: Countryside Commission. Role	719'.06'142
Projects by local authorities. Organisation	719'.0942
Landscape conservatiuon	719
Landscape design	
Use of plants	716
Use of water	714
Landscape design. Forests. Great Britain	715'.2
Landscape design. Gardens. England	
1528-ca 1640	712'.6'0942
Landscape design. Middle East	
Techniques — *Conference proceedings*	712'.3'0956
Landscape design. Urban regions	
Use of nature	712
Landscape graphic arts. Exhibits. LYC Museum and	
Gallery	
English landscape graphic arts. Holland, James & Moses,	
Marleen — *Catalogues*	760'.092'2

Figure 2
Classified
sequence

715'.2 — Forests. Landscape design. *Great Britain*
Crowe, *Dame* **Sylvia.** The landscape of forests
and woods / [by] Sylvia Crowe. — London :
H.M.S.O., [1978]. — 47p : ill(chiefly col),
map ; 28cm. — (Forestry Commission.
Booklets ; 44)
ISBN 0-11-710186-9 Pbk : £3.50

(B79-21125)

4.4 It will be noted that, in the classified sequence, the classification numbers are followed by headings in words. These are called *feature headings*. They are a "translation" of the classification number and are intended to guide a user who is browsing through the classified sequence.

Figure 3
Classified
sequence with
feature headings

712'.6 — New gardens. Planning. *Amateurs'* ←
    manuals
Davidson, Keir, *b.1952?.* Simple garden
    construction. — London : Ward Lock, Sept.
    1979. — [96]p. — (Concorde books)
    ISBN 0-7063-5815-5 : £3.95 : CIP entry
    ISBN 0-7063-5814-7 Pbk : £2.50
                                        (B79-21856)

712'.6'09 — Gardens, to 1977 ←
    King, Ronald, *b.1914.* The quest for paradise : a
    history of the world's gardens / [by] Ronald
    King ; with an introduction by Anthony
    Huxley. — Weybridge : Whittet Books Ltd :
    Windward ; [Leicester] ([Euston St., Freemen's
    Common, Aylestone Rd, Leicester LE2 7SS]) :
    [Distributed by WHS Distributors], 1979. —
    288p : ill(chiefly col), 3 facsims(2 col), plans,
    ports ; 31cm.
    Bibl.: p.280. — Index.
    ISBN 0-905483-10-3 : £9.95 : CIP rev.
                                        (B79-09681)

712'.6'0942 — Gardens. Landscape design. *England,*←
    1528-ca 1640
    Strong, Roy. The Renaissance garden in
    England / [by] Roy Strong. — London :
    Thames and Hudson, 1979. — 240p : ill,
    facsims, plans, ports ; 27cm.
    Index.
    ISBN 0-500-01209-1 : £12.00
                                        (B79-21857)

712'.6'094436 — Gardens. *France. Paris, 1898-1927.*←
    Illustrations
    Atget, Eugène. Atget's gardens : a selection of
    Eugène Atget's garden photographs / [selected
    and with text by] William Howard Adams ;
    introduction by Jacqueline Onassis ... —
    London : Gordon Fraser Gallery, 1979. —
    120p : chiefly ill, port ; 26cm.
    ISBN 0-86092-037-2 Pbk : £4.95 : CIP rev.
                                        (B79-13042)

4.5 Users may sometimes seek a document by its author or title. It is therefore necessary to include a sequence of entries under author and title headings. These entries are usually abbreviated and include a reference to the appropriate classification number where a full description may be found. The sequence is thus often referred to as the author/title index. Below are two extracts from the author/title index to an issue of the *British national bibliography*.

Figure 4
Author/title
index

Crouse, William Harry. The auto book. 2nd ed.
  McGraw-Hill. £11.20 629.28822 (B79-18471)
                              ISBN 0-07-014560-1
Crow, David Richard. Principles and applications of
  electrochemistry. 2nd ed. *Chapman and Hall etc.. £4.95*
  541.37 (B79-25718)   ISBN 0-412-16020-x
Crow, Harte C. Case studies in ultrasound. (Bartrum, Royal
  J). *Saunders. £14.95* 617.550754 (B79-21011)
                              ISBN 0-7216-1553-8
Crowe, John H. Dry biological systems. *Academic Press.*
  £12.00 574.1 (B79-15402)   ISBN 0-12-198080-4
Crowe, Percy Robert. Concepts in climatology. *Longman.*
  £6.50 551.6 (B79-13733)   ISBN 0-582-30013-4
Crowe, *Dame* Sylvia. The landscape of forests and woods. ←
  H.M.S.O. £3.50 715.2 (B79-21125)
                              ISBN 0-11-710186-9
Crowley, Aleister.
  The complete astrological writings of Aleister Crowley.
  Duckworth. £3.95 133.5 (B79-13284)
                              ISBN 0-7156-1331-6

Landscape Institute. *South East Chapter.* Landscape design
  for the Middle East. *RIBA Publications for the South
  East Chapter of the Landscape Institute. £6.50*
  712.30956 (B79-16805)   ISBN 0-900630-68-x
Landscape into art. (Clark, Kenneth, *Baron Clark, b.1903*)
  New ed.. *J. Murray. £3.95* 758.1094 (B79-20254)
                              ISBN 0-7195-3610-3
Landscape of forests and woods. (Crowe, *Dame* Sylvia). ←
  H.M.S.O. £3.50 715.2 (B79-21125)
                              ISBN 0-11-710186-9
Landscape painting. (Jeffares, Bo). *Phaidon. £5.95 : CIP rev.*
  758.109 (B79-09698)   ISBN 0-7148-1985-9
Landscapes : catalogue of an exhibition held at the LYC
  Museum and Art Gallery. (Holland, James). *Banks,
  Brampton, Cumbria CA8 2JH : LYC Museum and Art
  Gallery. £0.20* 760.0922 (B79-14893)
Lane, Edward William. An account of the manners and
  customs of the modern Egyptians written in Egypt
  during the years 1833-1835. *115 Bayham St., NW1 0AL
  : East-West Publication etc.. Unpriced* 962.03
  (B79-14316)   ISBN 0-85692-009-6
Lane, Margaret, *b.1907*. A country calendar, and other
  writings. (Thompson, Flora). *Oxford University Press.*
  £5.95 : CIP entry 942.2708230924 (B79-24142)
                              ISBN 0-19-211753-x

Note the author and title entries for the book on the landscape of forests and woods featured in Figure 2 above.

5   Since BNB wished to use data in machine-readable form as the source of entries in the national bibliography it was clearly desirable that entries for the subject index should be amenable to computer production from data held in the machine-readable file.

6   Because no existing computer-manipulated systems were suitable it was necessary to develop a new system which it was thought should possess certain features:

i) It should state the whole of a component subject under each lead term, ie, each entry should be co-extensive with the subject.

ii) Since the MARC record carries class numbers from more than one classification scheme the index should be independent of any classification scheme.   Thus the order of terms in the heading would not be derived from any one scheme.

iii) The system should make full use of the computer's ability to reduce human effort. Although the indexer should be expected to provide the terms from which the entry should be constructed, and determine their order, he should not be expected to write out the actual entries.

iv) Each of the entries should be equally meaningful to the user, who should be able to interpret the entries correctly with a minimum of instruction in how to read the index.

The system eventually developed is PRECIS.

7   *Citation order*

7.1   In developing the new system it was necessary to find a method which could be used as a basis for determining an order of terms in the headings (citation order), which would permit the computer to generate a full set of entries without disturbing the meaning, and which would also enable different indexers to achieve the prescribed order consistently.

7.2   The usual approach has been to attempt to set down the terms in an order which reflects their relative significance, the most significant being placed first and so on.

7.3   Over the years various significance orders have been established. However, these have been developed for single entry systems, ie, ones in which an entry is made under only one term—the one placed first. It was found that the various significance formulae only occasionally led to meaningful index entries after the terms had been manipulated by the computer so that each term in turn came into the lead position.

7.4   Significance order is important only in a single entry system, where an entry is made only under the term cited first, the other terms

17

generating references. However, as noted above, the proposed new system was to be a multiple entry system, with a full entry under each term. It was thus possible to abandon the idea of significance order as a basis for determining the order of terms and a new basis was sought.

7.5 A basis for the order of terms was eventually found in a new principle of "context dependency". This context dependent order has an obvious resemblance to the way in which a sentence is constructed, though it has no resemblance to the solutions derived from significance order. For an imaginary (!) subject the order of terms in PRECIS would be:

In a	
LONDON	Location
SUBURB	Part of location
a	
POLICEMAN	Key system (Object of action)
was	
KICKED	Action
by a	
HORSE	Agent

8 PRECIS is not computer produced in the sense in which this phrase is sometimes used. There are experimental systems in which the computer counts the incidence of words in an abstract, generating index entries automatically under the most frequently used words. In PRECIS the terms are selected and arranged into an initial order by human intellectual effort: the role of the computer is to eliminate the clerical work, and the attendant risk of error, in manipulating the selected terms so that each significant term will appear in turn as the lead whilst preserving its context. PRECIS is thus a *computer assisted* system.

9 The terms are assembled into order using a system of *role operators*, and a system of *manipulation codes* instructs the computer as to how the terms are to be manipulated in order to provide the actual entries.

10 The version of PRECIS here presented is a refinement of the original system and is known as PRECIS II. It was adopted by BNB in 1974 and by ANB in 1975.

18

11 *Assignment*

Students should examine a recent annual volume of the *British national bibliography* or *Australian national bibliography* and ensure that they understand the structure of a classified catalogue as exemplified by these publications.

PART I

SYNTAX

UNIT 1

1 *PRECIS entry format*

1.1 A string of terms organised into a context-dependent order can be shown diagramatically:

$$A > B > C > D$$

ie the author has considered D in the context of C, C in the context of B and B in the context of A. Put another way we can say that each term is context-dependent upon the term(s) to its left, and sets the term(s) to its right in their wider context. This may be clearer if we consider a string of words:

Great Britain > Secondary schools > Teachers > Remuneration

in which 'Secondary schools' is set in context by 'Great Britain' whilst itself establishing the context for 'Teachers' which in turn establishes the context for 'Remuneration'.

1.2 The extent to which the entries in an index are capable of conveying their message clearly depends upon the extent to which this relative order of words can be maintained. However, maintaining this order throughout a series of entries in which each word in turn appears as the lead presents problems. For example:

$$A - B - C - D$$

The term C is related in two ways: to A and B on its left and to D on its right:

$$\boxed{A.B} \longleftarrow \bigcirc C \longrightarrow \bigcirc D$$

In a single-line entry format it is impossible to represent this two way relationship in all the entries, eg,

$$C - D - A - B$$

PRECIS therefore employs a two-line entry structure:

which makes it possible to represent simultaneously the relationship of C to the wider terms (A and B) and the narrower term (D).

1.3   The three parts of a typical PRECIS entry are:

LEAD		QUALIFIER

DISPLAY

a)   The *lead position* is occupied by the filing term, ie the term which serves as the user's access point to the index.

b)   The *qualifier position* is occupied by the terms which set the lead in its wider context.

c)   The *display position* is occupied by those terms which are context-dependent on the lead.

1.4   Layout

The lead term is to be given in capital letters (in a printed index it is in bold type). The display is indented two spaces from the left. If the display or the qualifier occupies more than one line, the second and subsequent lines are indented a further six spaces (ie eight altogether) for the qualifier and a further two (ie four altogether) for the display. Examples:

PEAK DISTRICT. Derbyshire
   Geology
SURFACE COATING. Effect on bond resistance. Concrete beams.
         Structural components
   Corrosion inhibitors
SOUTH AUSTRALIA
   Port Adelaide. Freight transport. Shipping. Containers services.
Note that although terms are separated by a full stop (or sometimes other punctuation) no full stop appears after the final term in qualifier or display.

2   *Production of entries*

2.1   The production of PRECIS index entries in the standard format depends upon a sequence of operations whereby the terms from a PRECIS string are in turn 'shunted' through the lead position. This operation can be demonstrated if we consider the entries for the following string

(0) Great Britain
(1) secondary schools
(p) teachers
(2) remuneration

2.2 This string is marshalled into the display position, that is the lead position and the qualifier position are as yet unoccupied.

Great Britain Secondary schools Teachers Remuneration

The computer begins its operation by shunting the first of these terms into the lead position, leaving the remainder of the string in the display. This gives us the first entry:

Great Britain	

Secondary schools. Teachers. Remuneration

The lead term, 'Great Britain', is next shunted across into the qualifier and is replaced by the term from the front of the display, 'Secondary schools':

Secondary schools	Great Britain

Teachers. Remuneration

This operation is continued until each term in the display has been transferred to the lead position. Thus the two remaining entries for this example would be:

Teachers	Secondary Schools. Great Britain

Remuneration

and

Remuneration	Teachers. Secondary schools. Great Britain

2.3 The above set of entries demonstrates the *standard entry format*. Variations from it can, however, occur and are considered at various points later in this Workbook. Moreover, the generation of entries is not altogether as mechanical as this example might suggest. For example, in this case each term in turn appeared as a lead term. In practice the decision as to whether or not any term should appear in the lead is, together with other decisions, at the discretion of the indexer. These decisions, and the conventions by which they are indicated, are explained in section 4 of this unit.

3 *Filing*

3.1 If, in a PRECIS index, a number of entries appear under the same lead terms, they are sub-arranged by the qualifier, eg

LIBRARIES. Canberra
  Stock: Books in German language — *Union lists*
LIBRARIES. Schools. Australia
  Role in education
LIBRARIES. Victoria
  Inter-library loans — *Directories*

3.2 If two or more entries have the same lead term *and* qualifier, only the display line is printed for the second and subsequent entries, eg

LIBRARIES. Canberra
  Stock: Books in German language — *Union lists*
LIBRARIES. Melbourne
  Personnel. Recruitment
  Stock: Books in German language — *Union lists*
LIBRARIES. Schools. Australia
  Role in education
LIBRARIES. Victoria
  Inter-library loans — *Directories*

3.3 A reproduction of a page from the subject index to the *British national bibliography* also appears in the introductory matter to this Workbook.

4 *Conventions indicating the appearance of terms in the entry*
  √   Term to appear as lead
  √(LO) Term to appear as lead only
  (NU)   Not up

25

(ND)	Not down
(sub n)	Substitute for n higher terms
$v	Downwards reading connective
$w	Upwards reading connective
x	First term in a distinct theme
y	Subsequent term in a distinct theme
z	Term common to all themes

4.1 √ Term to appear as lead

Subject The control of insect pests

String (1) pésts
       (q) insects
       (2) control

Entries PESTS
           Insects. Control
           INSECTS. Pests
           Control

4.2 √(LO) Lead only

Subject Clause relationships in the Iatmul language
           (a New Guinean language)

String (1) Néw Guinean languages (LO)
       (q) Iátmul language
       (p) clause relationships

Entries NEW GUINEAN LANGUAGES
           Iatmul language. Clause relationships
           IATMUL LANGUAGE
           Clause relationships

4.3 (NU) Not up. Term not printed when the string is read from bottom to top (=when a lower term is in the lead), ie term printed in display, but not as a qualifier.

Subject Teaching girls in high schools

String (1) high schools
       (p) students (NU)
       (q) girls
       (2) téaching

Entries HIGH SCHOOLS
           Students. Girls. Teaching

STUDENTS. High schools
    Girls. Teaching.
GIRLS. High schools
    Teaching
TEACHING. Girls. High schools

(ND) has the equivalent effect when a higher term is in the lead: term printed as a qualifier, but not in display.

4.4 Substitution. The simplest way to re-phrase part of an entry is to write a substitute phrase which, being inserted into a string, replaces a stated number of higher terms *whenever a lower term comes into the lead*. Substitute phrases are preceded by an appropriate role operator AND a conventional sign—(sub n) where n is a number between 1 and 9 inclusive which shows how many terms should be suppressed and replaced by the substitute.

   Subject   The planning of medical research
    String   (2) medicine
            (p)   research
  (sub 2) (2) medical research
            (2) planning
  Entries MEDICINE
          Research. Planning
         PLANNING. Medical research

Without substitution the final entry would be:
         PLANNING. Research. Medicine
which might signify *either* The planning of medical research, *or* Research into medical planning.

4.5 $w Upwards connective
    String   (1) lubricating oils
            (p)   contaminants
            (q)   water
would produce as the final entry:
         WATER. Contaminants. Lubricating oils
This, however, is ambiguous: it could be interpreted as *either* lubricating oils as contaminants of water, *or* water as a contaminant of lubricating oils. However, by incorporating a connective—the preposition "of"—into the string we can clarify the final entry.

String   (1) lubricating oils
         (p) contaminants $w of
         (q) water
Entries LUBRICATING OILS
           Contaminants: Water
           CONTAMINANTS. Lubricating oils
           Water
           WATER. Contaminants of lubricating oils

Note that a connective coded $w is printed only when the string is being read in an upwards order, ie when the term to which it is attached is in the qualifier position.

String   (1) electric cookers
         (2) installation $w of
         (p) costs

Reading the string upwards: Costs, Installation of electric cookers

Entries ELECTRIC COOKERS
           Installation. Costs
           INSTALLATION. Electric cookers
           Costs
           COSTS. Installation of electric cookers

4.6 $v Downwards connective
   String   (0) South Africa
           (2) reading $v by
           (3) children
   Entries SOUTH AFRICA
           Reading by children
           READING. South Africa
           By children
           CHILDREN. South Africa
           Reading

Note that a connective coded $v is printed only when the string is being read in downwards order, ie when the term to which it is attached is in the display position or in the lead.

   String   (0) New York
           (2) educational visits $v by
           (3) children

Reading the string downwards: New York, Educational visits by children.

   Entries NEW YORK
           Educational visits by children

EDUCATIONAL VISITS. New York
    By children
CHILDREN. New York
    Educational visits

The format of the final entry in each of the two examples above is associated with the operator (3). The effect is known as predicate transformation and will be discussed in a later unit.

4.7 It is possible, and not unusual, to have both upwards and downwards connectives attached to the one term.

String   (1) children
            (2) réscue $v by $w of
            (3) dógs
Entries CHILDREN
            Rescue by dogs
          RESCUE. Children
            By dogs
          DOGS
            Rescue of children

Note that the downwards connective is written in the string before the upwards connective.

5 *Checking exercise 1*

When you think you understand the material in this unit work through the exercise which follows, and when you think you have arrived at a correct set of answers turn to the model answers at the back of the Workbook and compare them with your answers. If the model answer for any item differs from your solution work through the item again to see where you went wrong.

Write out the entries which would be produced from the following strings. These "nonsense" strings are intended to help you become conversant with the entry formats in PRECIS. Role operators would normally appear in the parentheses to the left of each term but have been omitted. Don't worry about them here.

1. ( ) cát	2. ( ) cat	3. ( ) cát
( ) dóg	( ) dóg	( ) dóg (NU)
( ) hén	( ) hén	( ) hen
( ) pig	( ) pig	( ) pig

4. ( ) cát
   ( ) dóg (ND)
   ( ) hẹn
   ( ) píg

5. ( ) cát
   ( ) dóg (LO)
   ( ) hẹn
   ( ) píg

6. ( ) cát
   ( ) dog
   ( ) hẹn $w of
   ( ) píg

7. ( ) cát
   ( ) dog
   ( ) hẹn $v by
   ( ) píg

8. ( ) cát
   ( ) dog
   ( ) hẹn $v by $w of
   ( ) píg

9. ( ) cát
   ( ) dóg $w on
   ( ) hẹn $v by $w of
   ( ) píg

10. ( ) cát
    ( ) dóg
(sub 2) ( ) fly
    ( ) hẹn
    ( ) píg

30

UNIT 2

Differences (Operators h−o, and d)

1   Any compound term, eg East Africa, vegetable oils, sour milk, or reinforced concrete bridges, consists of two elements:
   i)   Focus
   ii) One or more differences

1.1   Focus—that part of a compound term which specifies the conceptual class to which it belongs. In PRECIS the focus will always be an *entity* or an *activity*.

1.2   Difference—that part of a compound term which has a qualifying function. It will qualify either the focus or another difference.

1.3   In the terms above (East Africa, vegetable oils, sour milk, reinforced concrete bridges) the focus in each case is: Africa, oils, milk and bridges.   East, vegetable, sour and concrete are differences which qualify their respective foci. Reinforced, however, does not qualify its focus but the accompanying difference; it relates not to bridges but to concrete.

1.3.1   A difference which qualifies a focus is a *direct difference*.

1.3.2   A difference which qualifies another difference is an *indirect difference*.

1.3.3   A difference which is required as a lead (ie under which it is desired to make an entry) is a *lead difference*.

1.3.4   A difference which is not required as a lead is a *non-lead difference*.

1.3.5 A difference which is to be printed in parentheses when in the display or qualifier position is a *parenthetical difference*.

1.3.6 Codes

	Non-lead	Lead
Direct	h	i
Indirect	k	m
Parenthetical	n	o

2 *Notes*

2.1 Input order
Preceding differences are always written in the string in inverted order, eg "Re-inforced concrete bridges" as

    bridges $i concrete $m re-inforced

2.2 Output order
Preceding differences are always output in index entries in natural language order; inverted phrases *NEVER* appear in PRECIS entries,

    eg Re-inforced concrete bridges

3 *Format*

3.1 When any other term is in the lead the differenced concept is stated in full in the appropriate part of the entry.

3.2 When part (but not all) of the differenced concept is lead the differenced concept is stated in full as the first element in display.

3.3 When all the differenced concept is in the lead the differenced concept is *not* repeated as first element in display.

3.4 Example—Input order, output order and format of a differenced concept.

    Subject Welding of austentitic steel pipes in boilers

                          differenced concept

    String (1) boilers
            (p) pipes $i steel $m austentitic   *[differenced concept:*
            (2) welding   *input]*

Entries BOILERS
  Austentitic steel pipes. Welding
  PIPES. Boilers
  Austentitic steel pipes. Welding
  STEEL PIPES. Boilers
  Austentitic steel pipes. Welding
  AUSTENTITIC STEEL PIPES. Boilers
  Welding
  WELDING. Austentitic steel pipes. Boilers

The *first and last entries* show the differenced concept, output in natural language order, appearing in the appropriate part of the entry when another term is in the lead.

The *second and third entries* show part of the differenced concept in the lead and the differenced concept, stated in full and in natural language order, as the first element of the display.

The *fourth entry* shows the differenced concept in full in the lead.

4 *Non-lead direct difference* $h
Subject Feeding habits of common birds
String (1) birds $h common
  (p) habits
  (2) feeding
Entries BIRDS
  Common birds. Habits. Feeding
  HABITS. Common birds
  Feeding
  FEEDING. Habits. Common birds

5 *Lead direct difference* $i
Subject The conservation of weatherboard homesteads in Victoria
String (0) Victoria
  (1) homesteads $i weatherboard
  (2) conservation
Entries VICTORIA
  Weatherboard homesteads. Conservation
  HOMESTEADS. Victoria
  Weatherboard homesteads. Conservation
  WEATHERBOARD HOMESTEADS. Victoria
  Conservation
  CONSERVATION. Weatherboard homesteads. Victoria

33

Two lead direct differences together:

    (1) figurines $i portrait $i clayware

The $i shows that each of these differences directly qualifies the focus "figurines". In response to these codes each difference is attached *in turn* to the focus when the lead is being constructed:

> FIGURINES
>> Clayware portrait figurines
>
> PORTRAIT FIGURINES
>> Clayware portrait figurines
>
> CLAYWARE FIGURINES
>> Clayware portrait figurines

6 *Non-lead indirect difference* $k

    Subject The manufacture of high voltage electric cables in Canada

    String   (0) Canada

               (1) cables $i electric $k high voltage

               (2) manufacture

    Entries CANADA
>> High voltage electric cables. Manufacture
>
> CABLES. Canada
>> High voltage electric cables. Manufacture
>
> ELECTRIC CABLES. Canada
>> High voltage electric cables. Manufacture

7 *Lead indirect difference* $m

    Subject Re-inforced concrete bridges on narrow gauge railways

    String   (1) railways $i narrow gauge

               (p) bridges $i concrete $m re-inforced

    Entries RAILWAYS
>> Narrow gauge railways. Re-inforced concrete bridges
>
> NARROW GAUGE RAILWAYS
>> Re-inforced concrete bridges
>
> BRIDGES. Narrow gauge railways
>> Re-inforced concrete bridges
>
> CONCRETE BRIDGES. Narrow gauge railways
>> Re-inforced concrete bridges
>
> RE-INFORCED CONCRETE BRIDGES. Narrow gauge railways

8 *Parenthetical difference*

These operators are to be used in situations which require the addition of a qualifying phrase within parentheses. Concepts which need to be qualified in this way will be encountered mainly in sociology and education, where a particular attribute may lack a sufficiently precise definition until the measure used in its determination has been named.

8.1 Lead parenthetical difference

Subject Intelligence of infants as measured by the Wechsler Scale
Clearly this is *not* a document on the Wechsler Scale as such, nor is it about techniques of measurement, so that "Wechsler Scale" is a qualifier of the term intelligence: the document is about intelligence *as measured by the Wechsler Scale.*

String (1) infants
(p) intelligence $o Wechsler Scale

Entries INFANTS
Intelligence (Wechsler Scale)
INTELLIGENCE (Wechsler Scale). Infants
WECHSLER SCALE. Intelligence. Infants

8.2 Non-lead parenthetical difference

If the parenthetical difference is not required as a lead it should be prefixed by the code $n

eg (p) intelligence $n Wechsler Scale

The final entry in the example above would then be dropped.

Note that the parentheses are produced automatically in response to the code $n or $o; it is not necessary for the indexer to write them in the string.

9 *Date as difference*

9.1 Notes

a) Periods of time are described numerically rather than verbally, ie, '1837-1901' rather than 'Victorian'; '1701-1800' rather than 'eighteenth century'.

b) Dates should attach as low in the string as the subject allows.

c) If a date is used in conjunction with other differences it should be cited as the final difference.

9.2 Format

i) When the concept with which the date is associated is stated in

35

full, either in qualifier or display—the date is printed *in italics* immediately after the focus and is preceded by a comma.

ii) Part of the concept with which the date is associated appears in the lead—all of the concept will appear as the first element in the display (see para 3.2) and the date is printed *in italics* immediately after the focus and is preceded by a comma.

iii) All of the concept with which the date is associated appears in the lead—date is printed *in italics* as the first element in the display.

9.3 Examples

Subject The restoration of 16th century timber houses in London

String (0) Lóndon

(1) hóuses $i timber $d 1501-1600

(2) réstoration

Entries LONDON

Timber houses, *1501-1600*. Restoration

HOUSES. London

Timber houses, *1501-1600*. Restoration

TIMBER HOUSES. London

1501-1600. Restoration

RESTORATION. Timber houses, *1501-1600*. London

If an entry contains a phrase constructed out of terms and connectives, and one of these terms has a date attached, then the date is written at the end of the phrase.

Subject The astronomical observation of the eclipse of the sun in 1973

String (1) Sún

(2) eclipses $d 1973 $w of

(2) astronomical observation

Entries SUN

Eclipses, *1973*. Astronomical observation

ECLIPSES. Sun

1973. Astronomical observation

ASTRONOMICAL OBSERVATION. Eclipses of sun, *1973*

10 *Place as difference*

10.1 Place is to be used as a difference only when both of the following conditions are satisfied:

a) it defines an action or entity in terms of its place of origin

b) the action or entity so defined is "exportable" ie is capable of appearing in several contexts.

Thus:

      (1) wines $i French

is valid, since these may occur in different locational contexts.

10.2 Examples

    Subject The consumption of French wines in Canada

    String   (0) Canada

               (1) wines $i French

               (2) consumption

    Entries CANADA

               French wines. Consumption

           WINES. Canada

               French wines. Consumption

           FRENCH WINES. Canada

               Consumption

However:

        (1) castles $i Welsh

is invalid since castles are not exportable. This topic should be coded:

        (0) Wales

        (1) castles

10.3 This convention makes it possible to distinguish between different subjects which are made up from the same set of basic concepts. For example:

    String   (0) Great Britain

               (1) cinema films

               (2) distribution

    Entries GREAT BRITAIN

               Cinema films. Distribution

           CINEMA FILMS. Great Britain

               Distribution

           DISTRIBUTION. Cinema films. Great Britain

ie the distribution of cinema films in Great Britain regardless of the country of origin.

    String   (1) cinema films $i British

               (2) distribution

    Entries CINEMA FILMS

               British cinema films. Distribution

BRITISH CINEMA FILMS
Distribution
DISTRIBUTION. British cinema films
ie the distribution of British cinema films in any country.

We can, of course, specify also the distribution of British cinema films in one country:

    (0) France
    (1) cinema films $i British
    (2) distribution

11 *Prepositional phrases as differences*

11.1 So far we have been concerned with compound terms in which the qualifying word is an adjective or a noun acting as an adjective, for example:

> *woollen* blankets
> *concrete* bridges

However, in some instances the qualifying term may be a prepositional phrase, for example:

> welfare services *for children*
> documents *on Uganda*

Compound terms such as these pose a problem because the focus precedes the difference, and in order to code such terms successfully it is necessary to "twist" the meaning of the operators by treating the difference which follows the preposition as though it were the focal term, ie

> children $i welfare services for
> Uganda $h documents on

giving entries:

> CHILDREN
>   Welfare services for children
> WELFARE SERVICES FOR CHILDREN

and

> UGANDA
>   Documents on Uganda

11.2 A prepositional phrase may include two differences, eg

> Secondary schools for aboriginal students

String   students $i aboriginal $m secondary schools for
Entries STUDENTS
>   Secondary schools for aboriginal students

38

12 *Rules of differencing*

12.1 Do not difference a property or part by the entity or action which possesses it, eg
>   (1) soils
>   (p) acidity
>   *not* (1) acidity $i soils

However, a whole may be differenced by its part or property, eg
>   (1) soils $i acid
>   (1) cars $i two-door

12.2 Do not difference a transitive action by the entity on which it is performed, eg
>   (1) libraries
>   (2) management
>   *not* (2) management $i library

However, an entity may be differenced by the name of the action which has been or is being performed on it, eg
>   (1) frames $i rivetted

12.3 Do not difference an intransitive action by the name of the entity which performs it, eg
>   (1) birds
>   (2) migration
>   *not* (2) migration $i birds

However, an entity may be differenced by the name of the intransitive action in which it is engaged, eg
>   (1) birds $i migrating

12.4 Do not difference a transitive action by the name of the agent which performs it, eg
>   (1) soils
>   (2) erosion $v by $w of
>   (3) winds
>   *not* (1) soils
>   (2) erosion $i wind

39

However, an agent may be differenced by the name of the action for which it is intended, eg

$\qquad$ (1) tóols $i cutting

13 *Checking exercise 2*

When you think you understand the material in this unit work through the exercise which follows, and when you think you have arrived at a correct set of answers turn to the model answers at the back of the Workbook and compare them with your answers. If the model answer for any item differs from your solution, work through the item again to see where you went wrong.

In this exercise, and all succeeding exercises, underline words which should be in italics.

Write out the entries which would be produced from the following strings. Role operators would normally appear in the parentheses to the left of each term but have been omitted. Don't worry about them here.

1.   ( ) United States
            ( ) tractors $i agricultural
            ( ) tariffs

2.   ( ) United States
            ( ) vehicles $i electric $m battery powered
            ( ) testing

3.   ( ) Western Australia
            ( ) gold
            ( ) mining $d 1893-1973

4.   ( ) Czechoslovakia
            ( ) shells $i steel $h cylindrical $i re-inforced
            ( ) manufacture

5.   ( ) Great Britain
            ( ) cables $i electric $k high-voltage $i insulated $m plastic
            ( ) manufacture

Write out the focus and differences for the compound terms given below, and show the entries which would be produced from a string which consisted of ( ) Australia, with the differenced term below. Assume a lead will be required on the focus and on each difference. For example:

Forest ecosystems

String ( ) Au̯stralia

( ) eċosystems $i forest

Entries AUSTRALIA

Forest ecosystems

ECOSYSTEMS. Australia

Forest ecosystems

FOREST ECOSYSTEMS. Australia

6. Tin mining industry

7. Lead-acid traction batteries (NB: Hyphenated words are treated as a single word.

8. Deciduous fruit trees

9. New dark blue brushed nylon party dresses

10. Counselling services for migrants

UNIT 3

Use of the main line operators 0–3

1 The terms selected to make up the index entry are written out in a vertical column, and collectively are referred to as a 'string'. The string is ordered according to the operators, one of which is assigned to each term. The operators are placed in front of the terms (in the case of main line operators and interposed operators) and are enclosed within parentheses.

2 *(0) Location*

2.1 Used to code place name when the relational link between a locality and any following concepts is simply one of 'geographical constraint'—ie a certain thing or event (the *located concept*) happened to occur in a particular area which played no obvious part in the events described.

>   (0) New South Wales
>   (1) locusts
>   (2) migration

2.2 Note that in some circumstances locality is coded (1). This will be discussed further in Unit 7: *Coding of locality names*.

3 *(1) Key system*

3.1 Central concept. Usually the agent of an intransitive action or the object of a transitive action (the entity upon which an action is performed).

3.1.1 Agent of an intransitive action

>   (1) reptiles
>   (2) hibernation

>   (1) liquids
>   (2) flow

3.1.2 Object of a transitive verb
>   (1) steel
>   (2) welding
>
>   (1) books
>   (2) cataloguing

In natural language the relationship between the key system and the action, in these two situations, is frequently conveyed by the preposition 'of', eg the hibernation of reptiles, the welding of steel.

3.2 However, *when the action represents an internal or physiological process, the performer of the action should be coded as the key system.*
>   (1) divers
>   (2) breathing
>
>   (1) dogs
>   (2) respiration

4 *(2) Action/Effect*
Used to code the concept which expresses what is done to the key system or what is done by the agent, or an effect upon the key system.

4.1 Actions
Note that these are preferably expressed in a form other than the gerund, eg 'maintenance' rather than 'maintaining', or 'management' rather than 'managing'. Sometimes, however, the '——ing' form is unavoidable.
>   (1) metal
>   (2) polishing
>
>   (1) paper industries
>   (2) management

4.2 Effects
>   (1) animals
>   (2) diseases

4.3 Phenomenon
Some terms appear to lie on the borderline between the notion of an entity and an action. Although these terms are not obviously derived

from verbs they invariably entail the idea of an activity, and it is difficult to disentangle the two concepts. For example, 'cricket' entails human beings in a specific activity. So also, though less obviously, do most subject names, for example 'chemistry', which entail an activity of study and research within the discipline. Such terms are therefore also coded (2). Terms such as 'social conditions' are also regarded as of this type.

    (2) cricket

    (1) high schools
    (2) cricket

4.4 In certain circumstances it is possible to have two actions in the same string. There are broadly three sets of circumstances in which this may occur.

    a) The second action expresses the collection, processing, evaluation or dissemination of information about a higher term.

    (0) Australia
    (1) uranium
    (2) mining $w of
    (2) research

    b) The second action expresses a change made to, or interference with, a higher term.

    (1) digestive system
    (2) diseases
    (2) drug therapy

    c) The second action expresses the origin or development of a higher concept.

    (0) Great Britain
    (1) schools of librarianship
    (p) curriculum subjects
    (q) PRECIS
    (2) teaching
    (2) initiation

The indexer needs to be alert to the possible need for a use of a substitute phrase or a connecting preposition where a second action relates not to the preceding action but to a yet higher term or to a combination of terms. Thus in the first of the examples above 'research' is related not simply to 'mining' but to 'mining of uranium'. Thus the entry:

    RESEARCH. Mining of uranium. Australia

is a more accurate expression of the subject than

5 Note that it is a mandatory condition that every string must include the operator (1) and/or the operator (2).

6 *(3) Agent/Aspects*

6.1 Agent of a transitive action
This is the most common case.
       (1) cřops
       (2) dǎmage $v by $w to
       (3) fřost

6.2 Intake upon which an action is performed
When a subject includes an action and an intake the former is coded (2) and the latter (3)
       (1) birds
       (2) digestion $v of $w by
       (3) gřain

6.3 This operator may also be used to code aspects—see para 7.10.

7 *Predicate transformation*

7.1 An important variation from the standard format is known as predicate transformation. It is triggered by the juxtaposition in a string of operators (2) and (3).
  String   (1) cřops
           (2) dǎmage $v by $w to
           (3) fřost
  Entries   CROPS
             Damage by frost
          DAMAGE. Crops
             By frost
          FROST
             Damage to crops

7.2 Predicate transformation is also triggered by other 'action-performer' combinations which are considered in a later unit.

7.3 As demonstrated in this example an agentive term, such as 'frost', behaves in a normal way so long as it remains in the display. However, when it moves into the lead it triggers a special effect. The computer, having noted that a term coded (3) is due to appear in the lead, checks for the presence of an action, ie a term coded (2). If such a term is present it is dropped into the display position, and if an upwards reading connective ($w) is present it draws down the next higher term (as in the example above).

7.4 It the name of the agent is treated as a class of agents which is followed by a dependent element coded (q) these terms are treated as a block before the name of the action is transposed by predicate transformation.

String   (1) submarines
           (2) location $v by $w of
           (3) aircraft
           (q) swordfish

Entries SUBMARINES
          Location by aircraft: Swordfish
          LOCATION. Submarines
          By aircraft: Swordfish
          AIRCRAFT
          Swordfish. Location of submarines
          SWORDFISH. Aircraft
          Location of submarines

7.5 If the agentive term is a focus accompanied by one or more differences, differencing procedures are carried out before the action is transposed by predicate transformation.

String   (1) rivers
           (2) pollution $v by $w of
           (3) effluents $i industrial

Entries RIVERS
          Pollution by industrial effluents
          POLLUTION. Rivers
          By industrial effluents
          EFFLUENTS
          Industrial effluents. Pollution of rivers
          INDUSTRIAL EFFLUENTS
          Pollution of rivers

7.6 Predicate transformation ensures consistent phrasing, and therefore collocation in the index, when the agent of an action (coded (3)) is also a *part* of a system upon which, or within the context of which, the action is performed, the system therefore being coded (1). For example, teachers in colleges of advanced education may be regarded as a part, or sub-system, of a college. A document on high school teachers in general would be coded quite simply:

    (1) high schools
    (p) teachers

producing the entries:

    HIGH SCHOOLS
      Teachers
    TEACHERS. High schools

However, a document on "The assessment of their students by teachers in colleges of advanced education" would be coded:

    (1) high schools
    (p) students
    (2) assessment $v by $w of
    (3) teachers

Predicate transformation ensures that the entry under *teachers* is phrased consistently with the entry for teachers above and will be collocated with it:

    TEACHERS. High schools
      Assessment of students

7.7 Predicate transformation also ensures that in this situation the agentive term (Teachers) is associated with the system of which it is a part (High schools).

7.8 Predicate transformation causes no problems in the index so long as the system identified as the agent is actually responsible for the action which appears as the next higher term in the string. However, although this is usually the case there are exceptions; in particular it should be noted that in some situations the term coded as agent is not responsible for the action which appears as the higher term in the string. Rather it is responsible for some other action which is not stated because it is implied in the name of the agent. For example in the string

    (1) population
    (2) growth
    (3) mathematical models

47

Mathematical models are not an agent of growth, yet this string produces the following entry under this term:

> MATHEMATICAL MODELS. Population
> Growth

But mathematical models are being considered in the context of an implied study of growth, not in the context of population, ie predicate transformation does not, in this situation, lead to a helpful entry.

7.9 We can avoid producing predicate transformation by practising an act of deception. If a second operator (2) is inserted into the string, with a blank field, the predicate transformation entry will be suppressed.

String   (1) population
            (2) growth
            (2)
            (3) mathematical models

Entries POPULATION
            Growth. Mathematical models
           GROWTH. Population
            Mathematical models
           MATHEMATICAL MODELS. Growth. Population

Although the second action term is a blank space it is accepted by the computer as though it were a data element and it is assigned to the appropriate position in the entry. However, because there is nothing there, and because it is not coded to lead, it has no effect *except to suppress predicate transformation* which would have been effected by the 'blank' being in the display position in the final entry.

7.10 The same device should be used when operator (3) is used to code aspects.

String   (2) education
            (2)
            (3) social aspects

Entries EDUCATION
            Social aspects
           SOCIAL ASPECTS. Education

This ensures collocation in the index when the 'aspects' term follows a term which does not represent an action.

String   (1) governments
           (p) accountability
(sub 2) (1) government accountability
           (3) social aspects

Entries GOVERNMENTS
        Accountability. Social aspects
     ACCOUNTABILITY. Governments
        Social aspects
     SOCIAL ASPECTS. Government accountability

8 *Stages in concept analysis and coding*

Subject: The training of skilled personnel in the British textile industries

8.1 Establish the action, if present
       (2) training

8.2 If the action is transitive, establish the object
       (1) skilled personnel
       (2) training

8.3 Since the object is part of another system, code these as whole and part
       (1) textile industries
       (p) skilled personnel
       (2) training

8.4 Establish the environment
       (0) Great Britain
       (1) textile industries
       (p) skilled personnel
       (2) training

8.5 Entries
     GREAT BRITAIN
       Textile industries. Skilled personnel. Training
     TEXTILE INDUSTRIES. Great Britain
       Skilled personnel. Training
     SKILLED PERSONNEL. Textile industries. Great Britain
       Training
     TRAINING. Skilled personnel. Textile industries. Great
        Britain

9 *Checking exercise 3*

When you think you understand the material in this unit work through the exercise which follows, and when you think you have arrived at a correct set of answers turn to the model answers at the back of the Workbook and compare them with your answers. If the model answer for any item differs from your solution, work through the item again to see where you went wrong.

Write out PRECIS strings, appropriate for the following items. For example:

Item Cooling of lasers using liquid hydrogen
String (1) lásers
  (2) cóoling $v by $w of
  (3) hýdrogen $i liquid

1. The distribution of silent cinema films in Great Britain in the 1920s*
2. The digestion of raw meat by dogs
3. Traffic congestion on roads in London
4. Social aspects of radicalism in France
5. Economic conditions in the clothing industry in Victoria
6. The hiring of small sailing boats
7. The administration of the education of physically handicapped children
8. Measurement of the mental development of children**
9. Investigation by accountants of the misappropriation of investment funds
10. Water conservation

*Enter "cinema films" in this form.
**Enter "Mental development" in this form.

Now write out the entries which would be produced by the following strings.

11.   (1) búildings
     (2) dámage $v by $w to
     (3) fróst

12.   (0) Néw York
     (1) mígrants $i Greek
     (2) edúcation

50

13.   (1) fruit trees
           (2) contamination $v by $w of
           (3) insecticides $i toxic

14.   (0) Europe
           (1) bridges $i concrete $m pre-stressed $h long
           (2) construction

15.   (0) Victoria
           (1) livestock
           (2) destruction $v by $w of
           (3) bushfires $d 1977

UNIT 4

The interposed operators p, q and r

1 *(p) Part/Property*

1.1 This operator is used to introduce the parts or properties of things or actions.

(1) cărs	(1) Jĕws	(1) tĕachers	(1) Brĭtish Columbia
(p) dŏors	(p) cŭstoms	(p) prŏfessionalism	(p) Vĭctoria

1.2 The operator can be introduced into a string after any of the main line operators discussed in the previous unit. It may be introduced as often as required, the onus being on the indexer to decide "which possesses what" and thus to ensure that terms are set out in their correct order. For example, the terms in the subject 'The strength of the hinges of car doors' should be set down as:

    (1) cărs
    (p) dŏors   (Part)
    (p) hĭnges   (Part of part)
    (p) strength   (Property of part of part)

1.3 The operator may also follow (q).

    (0) Lŏndon
    (1) căthedrals (NU)
    (q) St̆. Paul's Cathedral
    (p) ărchitectural features
    (q) wŏodwork

1.4 The operator is used to code various types of part/property relationships.

52

1.4.1 Parts, or sub-assemblies, of entities
       (1) aircraft
       (p) wings

1.4.2 Software components
       (1) railway services
       (p) timetables

1.4.3 Action which forms part of, or assists, another
       (2) sailing
       (p) tacking

1.4.4 Physical/Chemical properties
       (1) soils
       (p) acidity
ie properties which can be observed, tested and demonstrated.

1.4.5 Attributed properties
       (1) juries
       (p) impartiality
ie properties which are attributed but cannot be tested and demonstrated.

1.4.6 Inputs
       (1) motor cycles
       (p) petrol

1.4.7 Outputs
       (1) aircraft
       (p) noise

1.4.8 Properties of actions
       (1) advertising
       (p) costs

1.4.9 Sub-systems of a system
       (1) schools
       (p) libraries

2 *(r) Aggregates*
   eg collective nouns

2.1 Some examples:
(1) wólves   (1) wítches   (1) páintings   (1) shíps
(r) packs   (r) covens   (r) collections   (r) fleets

2.2 This makes possible the distinction between
                  (1) wólves
                  (2) béhaviour   ie the behaviour of individual wolves
and
                  (1) wólves
                  (r) packs
                  (2) béhaviour   ie the behaviour of wolves in packs

2.3 However, collective nouns have no value as a lead, and also need
to be demoted as collocating words.

2.3.1 It will be recalled that entries under a common lead term are
sub-arranged by the first word in the qualifier. Because a collective
noun has little value as a collocating word a substitute phrase is used so
that the collective noun does not become the first word in the qualifier.
                  (1) wólves
                  (r) packs
       (sub 2) (1) wolf packs
                  (2) béhaviour
     WOLVES   BEHAVIOUR. Wolf packs
       Packs. Behaviour
This achieves the following filing order:
               BEHAVIOUR. Animal packs
               BEHAVIOUR. Animals
               BEHAVIOUR. Dingo packs
               BEHAVIOUR. Dingoes
               BEHAVIOUR. Wolf packs
               BEHAVIOUR. Wolves
Not
               BEHAVIOUR. Animals
               BEHAVIOUR. Dingoes
               BEHAVIOUR. Packs. Animals
               BEHAVIOUR. Packs. Dingoes

BEHAVIOUR. Packs. Wolves
BEHAVIOUR. Wolves

3 *(q) Quasi-generic relationships*

3.1 In PRECIS a distinction is drawn between true generic relationships and quasi-generic relationships.

3.2 True generic relationships are *a priori* relationships. They:
    reflect aspects of the genus-species relationship;
    form part of the definition of a term;
    are permanent and not dependent on context;
    are handled in PRECIS by means of a reference.
      eg RODENTS
        See also
        MICE
The relationship can be shown diagramatically:

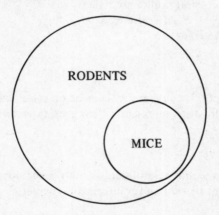

3.3 Quasi-generic relationships are *a posteriori* relationships. They:
    do not reflect aspects of the genus-species relationship;
    do not form part of the definition of a term;
    are not permanent but are context dependent;
    are handled in PRECIS by the operator (q).

(1) láboratory animals	(1) pésts	(1) péts
(q) míce	(q) míce	(q) míce

The relationship may be shown diagramatically:

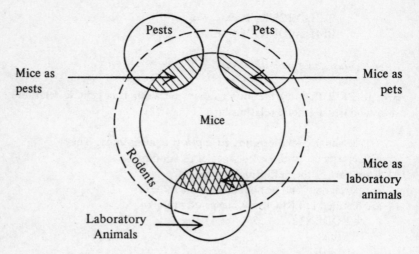

Mice as pests

Mice as pets

Mice as laboratory animals

Laboratory Animals

3.4 The distinction can be expressed by the following logical expressions:

True generic   ALL mice are rodents
Quasi-generic   SOME mice are pets

Consequently the reference:

RODENTS
  See also
    MICE

is valid and helpful because any document on mice will be relevant to a search for information on rodents. However, the reference:

PETS
  See also
    MICE

would not be valid and helpful because only some documents on mice would be relevant to a search for information on pets.

3.5 In display the operator (q) generates a colon in front of the term so coded.

Subject   Control of snails in the garden
String   (1) gárdens
            (p) pésts
            (q) snáils
            (2) control
Entries GARDENS
              Pests: Snails. Control

PESTS. Gardens
    Snails. Control
SNAILS. Pests. Gardens
    Control

3.6 The operator (q) 'quasi-generic' term is also used in three other situations:

3.6.1 to 'explain' a term which might otherwise give rise to an ambiguous reading

      (1) schools
      (p) curriculum subjects
      (q) woodwork

      (1) schools
      (p) buildings
      (p) architectural features
      (q) woodwork

the simple string

      (1) schools
      (p) woodwork

would be ambiguous.

3.6.1.1 Note that once a quasi-generic term has been introduced in this way it should, for the sake of consistency, be used in other related cases, eg

      (1) schools
      (p) curriculum subjects
      (q) mathematics

3.6.2 Homonyms also call for the operator (q). The method of distinguishing between them is to include in the string the term which describes the class to which the homonym belongs.

  (1) enclosure   (1) sports
  (q) fencing   (q) fencing

Note that, because we are in this case dealing with a true generic relationship, the name of the class should not be marked as a lead. References would be made:

ENCLOSURE   SPORTS
  See also   *See also*
    FENCING. Enclosure   FENCING. Sports

57

3.6.3 A special situation which is handled by the operator (q) occurs when a term represents a 'class-of-one', ie one named individual member of a class (a proper name). In this case the class term is included in the string in order to establish the context, and it may be used as a lead.

        (0) Victoria
        (1) historic homesteads
        (q) Tyntynder

Use of the class term as a lead achieves useful collocation in the index.

        HISTORIC HOMESTEADS. New South Wales
          Camden
        HISTORIC HOMESTEADS. Victoria
          Golf Hill
          Tyntynder

Note that a lower case c accompanies the tick over the 'class-of-one'.

3.6.3.1 Note that sometimes, to avoid tautology, the class term should be coded (NU).

        (0) Great Britain
        (1) cathedrals (NU)
        (q) Salisbury Cathedral

in order to secure the entry:

        SALISBURY CATHEDRAL. Great Britain

rather than:

        SALISBURY CATHEDRAL. Cathedrals. Great Britain

3.6.3.2 It may be necessary to suppress two higher terms. For example

        (0) Melbourne
        (1) cricket grounds (NU)
        (q) Melbourne Cricket Ground

This string will generate, under the final term, the entry:

        MELBOURNE CRICKET GROUND. Melbourne

However, we cannot code 'Melbourne' (NU) as under 'cricket grounds' if we wish to achieve, in the index, a sequence of entries sub-arranged by place, for example:

        CRICKET GROUNDS. Adelaide
          Adelaide Oval
          Salisbury Cricket Ground
        CRICKET GROUNDS. Melbourne
          Albert Park
          Melbourne Cricket Ground

CRICKET GROUNDS. Sydney
    Manly Cricket Ground
    Sydney Cricket Ground

If the place name was coded (NU) it would not print when 'Cricket grounds' is the lead term, and so the result would be an arrangement alphabetically by name of the ground, regardless of city:

CRICKET GROUNDS
    Adelaide Oval
    Albert Park
    Manly Cricket Ground
    Melbourne Cricket Ground
    Salisbury Cricket Ground
    Sydney Cricket Ground

3.6.3.3 We can retain the place name for the entry under 'Cricket grounds' yet suppress it from any subsequent entry, by substituting a blank.

    (0) Melbourne
    (1) cricket grounds
(sub 2) (1)
    (q) Melbourne Cricket Ground

This will produce the entries:

MELBOURNE
    Cricket grounds: Melbourne Cricket Ground
CRICKET GROUNDS. Melbourne
    Melbourne Cricket Ground
MELBOURNE CRICKET GROUND

3.7 Personal names are treated as a 'class-of-one' and should be 'context established' as described above, eg,

    (1) painters
    (q) Martens, Conrad

4 Students may sometimes encounter difficulty in deciding whether a particular relationship calls for the operator 'p' or the operator 'q'. Given that two terms are always involved—a higher term and a lower term, 'p' or 'q' being assigned to the lower term, and that A is the higher term and B the lower term—it will be helpful to ask the following questions:

4.1 Could B be a part or property of *any* specific A? If the answer is 'Yes' use operator 'p'; 'No' calls for operator 'q'.

4.2 Is B a specific member of the whole category A? If 'Yes' use operator 'q'; 'No' calls for operator 'p'.

4.3 For example 'Tacking' may be involved in *any* act of sailing and the correct analysis is therefore

        (2) sailing
        (p) tacking

However, a periodical is not part of any library stock in the sense in which 'parts' is used in PRECIS (eg, in this context, pages, bindings, etc). Periodicals is therefore a *type* of stock and is coded 'q'. Bearing in mind the rule that a concept may not be differenced by the whole of which it forms a part 'library stock' must be entered as two separate terms and the string is thus:

        (1) libraries
        (p) stock
        (q) periodicals

5 *Checking exercise 4*

When you think you understand the material in this unit, work through the exercise which follows, and when you think you have arrived at a correct set of answers turn to the model answers at the back of the Workbook and compare them with your answers. If the model answer for any item differs from your solution, work through the item again to see where you went wrong.

Write PRECIS strings appropriate for the following items. For example

  Item   Private collections of paintings in France
  String (0) France
        (1) paintings
        (r) private collections

1. Anatomy of the musculoskeletal system in cattle
2. Conservation of the sacred objects of aborigines
3. The breeding of Rough Collies in Scotland
4. The manufacture of decorative glassware bowls in Bohemia
5. Measurement of the noise of Concorde (the supersonic aircraft)
6. The herding of flocks of sheep by kelpies

7. The stained glass windows in Chartres Cathedral in France

8. Science in primary schools

9. The academic achievement of students in Australian Colleges of Advanced Education

10. Fashioning the blades of Stone Age cutting tools

Now write out the entries which would be produced by the following strings.

11.   (1) building sites
            (p) lifting equipment
            (q) cranes
            (p) safety

12.   (1) offices
            (p) digital computer systems
            (q) IBM system 360/40
            (2) programming

13.   (1) fish
            (r) shoals
  (sub 2) (1) fish shoals
            (2) detection $v by $w of
            (3) radar

14.   (0) Adelaide
            (1) art festivals
  (sub 2) (1)
            (q) Adelaide Festival $d 1978

15.   (1) vegetables
            (2) contamination $v by $w of
            (3) insecticides
            (q) organochlorine compounds

UNIT 5

Main line operators 4 and 6; some indexing problems

1 *(4) Viewpoint-as-form*

1.1 This operator is used to introduce the viewpoint of the author
where this has influenced his treatment of the subject, eg *Marxist viewpoint*. It causes the term which follows it to be printed in italics after a
hyphen, and it also triggers an inverted pattern when it appears in the
lead, ie terms from the qualifier position are printed in display.

1.2 Examples
    String (0) France
           (2) industrial relations
           (4) Roman Catholic viewpoints
    Entries FRANCE
           Industrial relations — *Roman Catholic viewpoints*
           INDUSTRIAL RELATIONS. France
           — *Roman Catholic viewpoints*
           ROMAN CATHOLIC VIEWPOINTS
           France. Industrial relations
    String (0) France
           (2) industrial relations
           (4) sociological perspectives
    Entries FRANCE
           Industrial relations — *Sociological perspectives*
           INDUSTRIAL RELATIONS. France
           — *Sociological perspectives*
           SOCIOLOGICAL PERSPECTIVES
           France. Industrial relations

62

String   (0) France
            (2) industrial relations
            (4) trade union viewpoints
Entries FRANCE
            Industrial relations *– Trade union viewpoints*
            INDUSTRIAL RELATIONS. France
            – Trade union viewpoints
            TRADE UNION VIEWPOINTS
            France. Industrial relations

Note that the "standard pattern" for the final entry for each of these strings would have placed 'France' and 'Industrial relations' in the qualifier, and in a different order, eg

        ROMAN CATHOLIC VIEWPOINTS. Industrial relations
        France

1.3 The author's viewpoint should only be included in a string when it has some part to play in assisting a user to select or reject a particular document. It will usually be found that stated viewpoints belong to one or other of the following categories:

a) the observer represents a field or discipline other than the one to which the concepts in the main theme belong (eg the first two examples above).

b) the observer concentrates upon a restricted aspect of the field to an extent likely to limit the usefulness of the document to readers who are not interested in the viewpoint presented (eg third example).

2 *(5) Sample populations/Study regions*
See below. This operator is discussed in the section on *Coding of locality names.*

3 *(6) Target/Form*

3.1 Target expresses the category of readers for whom a document is intended (cf DC19 ss 024). As a general rule if the target can be expressed by naming an action, this name is preferred to the name of the class of persons, eg "engineering" rather than "engineers".

String   (2) mathematics
            (6) engineering $h for
Entries MATHEMATICS
            – For engineering

63

ENGINEERING
 Mathematics – *For engineering*

3.2 Form is used in the usual documentary sense of "form of present-ation" (cf DC19's Table 1 of standard subdivisions)

Subject A walker's guide to Ben Nevis
String (0) Scotland
    (1) mountains
    (q) Ben Nevis
    (6) walkers' guides
Entries SCOTLAND
    Mountains: Ben Nevis – *Walkers' guides*
   MOUNTAINS. Scotland
    Ben Nevis – *Walkers' guides*
   BEN NEVIS. Mountains. Scotland
    – *Walkers' guides*
   WALKERS' GUIDES
    Scotland. Mountains: Ben Nevis

3.3 Target and form together

Target and form may occur together in the same string, and because each is introduced by the same operator no prescribed order is laid down. If the order of terms has no effect on the meaning of the entry it is recommended that target should precede form. However, care should be taken, since in some instances the relative position of target and form may change the meaning of the entry. For example the string

    (2) data processing
    (6) librarianship $h for
    (6) bibliographies

produces the entries

   DATA PROCESSING
    – *For librarianship – Bibliographies*
   LIBRARIANSHIP
    Data Processing – *For librarianship – Bibliographies*

which specifies the idea of a bibliography of those works on data pro-cessing which were written for librarians. However, the string

    (2) data processing
    (6) bibliographies
    (6) librarianship $h for

produces the entries

DATA PROCESSING
   - Bibliographies - For librarianship
LIBRARIANSHIP
   Data processing - *Bibliographies - For librarianship*
which expresses the idea of bibliographies, intended for librarians, of all
works on data processing.

3.4 One would not usually code a form of presentation term as a lead.
Clearly terms such as "Inquiry reports" or "Dictionaries" are not useful
lead terms. As a rule of thumb one could say that only when a form of
presentation implies a particular audience should it be considered as a
possible lead. Thus terms such as "climbers' guides", "Walkers' guides"
may be regarded as possibly useful lead terms.

4 *Some indexing problems*

4.1 Redundancy
We have already noted the use of a blank substitute to avoid unwanted
predicate transformation (see Unit 3, para 7.9) and to avoid tautology
(see Unit 4, para 3.6.3.2).

4.1.1 The question of redundancy arises in other situations. For
example:

       (0) Melbourne
       (1) secondary schools
       (p) curriculum subjects
       (q) English language
       (2) teaching
would give the following entry under Teaching:
   TEACHING. English language. Curriculum subjects. Secondary
              schools. Melbourne
The term 'Curriculum subjects' is redundant when an entry is made
under 'Teaching' because in this case the lead term implies the existence
of a curriculum.

4.1.2 The use of a substitution will avoid this redundancy.
         (0) Melbourne
         (1) secondary schools
         (p) curriculum subjects
         (q) English language
 (sub 2) (p) English language
         (2) teaching

65

This string will produce the following entry under Teaching:

TEACHING. English language. Secondary schools. Melbourne

4.2 Indirect object

If we add to the above subject a term designating to whom English is taught, eg, Teaching English language *to migrants* in secondary schools in Melbourne, we have two objects. 'English language' serves as the direct object and 'migrants' as the indirect object.

4.2.1 We have two problems:
   i) which object should be coded first, as a dependent element of secondary schools? and
   ii) how should the other object be coded?

4.2.2 The rule is to cite first the indirect object (ie, migrants) and to introduce the direct object with the operator (3). The string and entries for our subject will thus be as follows. Note the shedding of redundant terms when 'Teaching' is the lead term.

String	(0)	Melbourne
	(1)	sécondary schools
	(p)	stúdents (NU)
	(q)	mígrants
	(3)	cúrriculum subjects
	(q)	Énglish language
(sub 3)	(p)	English language to migrants
	(2)	téaching

Entries SECONDARY SCHOOLS. Melbourne
     Students: Migrants. Curriculum subjects: English
        language. Teaching
   STUDENTS. Secondary schools. Melbourne
     Migrants. Curriculum subjects: English language.
        Teaching
   MIGRANTS. Secondary schools. Melbourne
     Curriculum subjects: English language. Teaching
   CURRICULUM SUBJECTS. Migrants. Secondary schools.
        Melbourne
     English language. Teaching
   TEACHING.   English language to migrants.   Secondary
        schools. Melbourne

5 *Checking exercise 5*

When you think you understand the material in this unit, work through the exercise which follows, and when you think you have arrived at a correct set of answers turn to the model answers at the back of the Workbook and compare them with your answers. If the model answer for any item differs from your solution, work through the item again to see where you went wrong.

Write PRECIS strings appropriate for the following items. Use underlining to indicate italics. For example:

Item   The Australian special libraries directory
String   (0) Aŭstralia
         (1) spécial libraries
         (6) directories

1. Regulations for the lending of periodicals to students in academic libraries
2. A sociological study of military life
3. An inquiry report into the prices of spare parts for cars in Australia
4. The Royal Flying Doctor Service in New South Wales
5. Statistics for social scientists
6. The manufacture of thermally insulated hot water pipes
7. Anatomy for nurses
8. A union list of periodicals in London libraries
9. Medibank: a Trade Union viewpoint*
10. A bibliography of proceedings of conferences on Australian social welfare statistics

Write out the entries which would be produced by the following strings.

11. (0) Călifornia
    (1) gŏld fields
    (2) sŏcial conditions $d 1852
    (6) personal observations

12. (2) physics
    (6) secondary school texts
    (6) bibliographies

13. (0) Něw Zealand
    (1) unemployment
    (2) gŏvernment policies
    (4) sŏciological perspectives

14. (0) Nŏrthern Territory
    (1) ăborigines
    (p) lănd rights
    (4) mining company view-points

15. (0) Grĕat Britain
    (2) sport
    (6) conference proceedings

*Medibank was a health service in Australia

67

UNIT 6

Coding of locality names

1 When the name of a locality constitutes the principal or only entity in a subject it is, of course, coded (1)

> (1) Nèw Zealand

> (1) Nèw Zealand
> (p) Christchurch

> (1) Nèw Zealand
> (p) Christchurch
> (6) travel guides

In other cases, ie when further concepts are present in the subject, the correct coding of the place name depends on the factors considered in the remainder of this Unit.

2 When the relational link between a locality and any following concepts is one of 'geographical constraint' the place name is coded (0)

> (0) Mèlbourne
> (1) historic buildings
> (2) preservation

3 *Location as a geographical entity*

3.1 The location is coded (1) when a located concept coded (p) or (2) is a natural feature or phenomenon whose name does not imply an actual or intended use by man, eg

> (1) Victoria
> (p) coastal waters

> (1) Nòrway
> (2) winter $d 1963

3.1.1 Note, however, that this only applies so long as some other entity is not logically the key system, thus reducing locality to 'geographical constraint', eg

    (0) Switzerland
    (p) mountains
    (1) flowers

3.2 In all other cases where locality is a geographical entity it should be coded (0) and the located concept should be coded (1) or (2), eg

    (0) Italy
    (1) natural resources
    (q) rivers

In this example 'Italy' has been coded (0) on the grounds that 'natural resources' implies an actual or intended use by man.

4 *Location as a social, political or economic entity*

4.1 The location is coded (1) when the located concept represents or implies an action or activity which involves the entire community, eg

    (1) United States
    (2) politics

    (1) Great Britain
    (p) law

4.2 Typical concepts which meet this requirement, and the operators which introduce them, include:

(p) immigrants	(2) foreign relations
(p) imports	(2) immigration
(p) law	(2) politics
(p) population	(2) social conditions
(2) cultural relations	(2) social life
(2) economic conditions	

Although the first four of these concepts represent entities, coded (p), each of the first three necessarily entails, or is defined in terms of, an action, whilst the fourth represents the community itself.

4.3 In other cases where the location represents a social, political or economic entity, it should be coded (0), eg

    (0) Israel
    (1) passenger transport

69

        (0) Néw York City
        (1) négroes

4.4 A useful rule of thumb is that where English usage involves the preposition 'in' the operator (0) is usually called for, whereas 'of' usually calls for (1)

Phrase The population of Vienna
String   (1) Aústria
           (p) Viénna
           (p) pópulation
Phrase The education of migrants in Australia
String   (0) Aústralia
           (1) mígrants
           (2) edúcation

5. You should observe the following conventions:

5.1 For any city, town or region overseas the country should usually be included in the string
           (1) Húngary
           (p) Búdapest
           (6) travel guides
Exceptions may be made in the case of capital cities of major countries in which cases, to avoid congestion in the index, the relationship may be shown by a reference

CHINA   (1) Chína
   See also   rather than   (p) Péking
   PEKING

5.2 For any city, town or region in the home country of an indexing agency the State, County or Territory should be included in the string.
           (0) Victoria
           (p) Wímmera
           (1) sóil
           (2) erósion

           (0) Nórthamptonshire
           (p) Córby
           (1) steel industry
However, an exception to this convention may be made in the case of capital cities of states, counties or territories.

70

(0) Quebec
(1) theatres
(2) visits $v by $w to
(3) children

5.3 Observe also the convention, used in BNB and ANB, that when the home country is coded (0) it is not employed as a lead. This is to reduce the number of entries in the index under 'Great Britain' in the case of BNB and under 'Australia' in the case of ANB.

6 *Operator (5), Sample populations/Study regions*

This operator is used when a location, or a group of people, animals etc is not significant in itself but is used as a sample for an investigation from which to draw general conclusions.

6.1 In this case the sample is de-emphasised by being placed low in the string, and is preceded in the string by an appropriate term such as "study region", "sample population", etc. The term "study region", "sample population", or whatever term is used, is coded (5), the actual region or sample being coded (q).

6.2 Format
The operator (5) causes the term which follows to be printed in italics after a dash; the name of the region or sample is also italicised. This operator implements an inverted pattern when the term coded (5), or the dependent term coded (q), appears as a lead. Note, however, that it is most unusual for the term coded (5) to be employed as a lead.

6.3 Example
String (1) book trade
          (2) management
          (5) study region
          (q) Canada
Entries BOOK TRADE
            Management — *Study regions : Canada*
        MANAGEMENT. Book trade
           — *Study regions : Canada*
        CANADA. *Study regions*
           Book trade. Management

6.4   The operator (5) can be used to introduce concepts other than the names of localities. For example a document entitled "The anatomy of vertebrates" which explains in detail the parts of a dogfish, drawing attention to its typical vertebrate features, would call for the string:

        (1) v́ertebrates
        (p) ańatomy
        (5) study examples
        (q) dógfish

Note that the named example must be a kind or part of some concept which was specified or implied earlier in the string.

7   *Checking exercise 6*

When you think you understand the material in this unit, work through the exercise which follows, and when you think you have arrived at a correct set of answers turn to the model answers at the back of the Workbook and compare them with your own answers. If the model answer for any item differs from your solution, work through the item again to see where you went wrong.

Write PRECIS strings appropriate for the following items.   For example:

    Item   A guide to Bendigo (Indexing agency in Australia)
    String (1) Victoria
              (p) Béndigo
              (6) travel guides

  1. Shipwrecks in Chinese coastal waters
  2. The standards of living of Greek migrants in Melbourne, based on a study in Fitzroy
  3. A catalogue of New Zealand postage stamps (NB Postage stamps is entered as 'postage stamps' *not* stamps $i postage)
  4. Social conditions in Great Britain, c.1801-1900
  5. An inquiry report into the price of spare parts for cars in Australia
  6. A catalogue of nineteenth century English watercolour paintings
  7. Charts of British coastal waters
  8. A guidebook to the Grand Union Canal in Great Britain
  9. Social life in the rural areas of Greece
10. Sales of onions in Wales by itinerant salesmen from France

Write out the entries which would be produced by the following PRECIS strings.

11. (1) Cžechoslovakia
    (p) Pŕague
    (6) travel guides

12. (1) Iŕeland
    (p) rúral areas
    (2) sócial conditions

13. (0) Mélbourne
    (1) chíldren $i hospitals for (NU)
    (q) Róýal Children's Hospital

14. (1) Gŕeat Britain
    (2) climate $d c1801-1900

15. (1) Sýdney
    (p) pópulation
    (q) abórigines
    (2) ecónomic conditions
    (5) study regions
    (q) Rédfern

UNIT 7

Concept interlinks: Operators (s) and (t)

1 *Role definer:* Operator (s)
Used in three situations:

1.1 To define an action (ie a role) with which an agent is not usually
associated, eg the string
        (1) schools
        (2) administration $v by $w of
        (3) teachers
would not give entries which render accurately the subject "The role
of teachers in the administration of schools". Hence the operator (s) is
used to introduce a term which clarifies the otherwise doubtful relationship, and this term is accompanied by upwards and downwards connectives.

  String   (1) schools
           (2) administration
           (s) role $v of $w in
           (3) teachers
 Entries SCHOOLS
               Administration. Role of teachers
           ADMINISTRATION. Schools
               Role of teachers
           TEACHERS. Schools
               Role in administration

1.2 "Indirect agent"—Ranganathan's *tool phase*, ie where the agent is
used as a tool, or method, for carrying out an action.
The string

74

(1) dócuments
(2) indexing $v by $w of
(3) cómputer systems $i digital

would not give entries which render accurately the subject of "the application of digital computer systems in the indexing of documents". Hence the operator (s) is used to introduce some term, eg use *or* application, which is accompanied by upwards and downwards connectives:

String (1) dócuments
        (2) indexing $w of
        (s) application $v of $w in
        (3) cómputer systems $i digital

Entries DOCUMENTS
        Indexing. Application of digital computer systems
        INDEXING. Documents
        Application of digital computer systems
        COMPUTER SYSTEMS
        Digital computer systems. Applications in indexing
           of documents
        DIGITAL COMPUTER SYSTEMS
        Application in indexing of documents

1.3 "Indirect action"—Ranganathan's *influence phase* ie where a concept is not the agent of a direct and obvious action, but is agent only insofar as it influences some other concept, or has *implications* for it, eg

        (1) students
        (2) academic achievement $w of
        (s) influence $v of $w on
        (3) home environment

        (1) motor vehicles
        (p) stability $w of
        (s) effects $v of $w on
        (3) winds (LO)
        (q) sidewinds

        (1) developing countries
        (2) economic planning
        (s) implications $v of $w for
        (3) social change

1.3.1 Entries for string 1:
        STUDENTS
        Academic achievement. Influence of home environment

ACADEMIC ACHIEVEMENT. Students
Influence of home environment
HOME ENVIRONMENT
Influence on academic achievement of students

1.3.2 Entries for string 2:
MOTOR VEHICLES
Stability. Effects of sidewinds
WINDS
Sidewinds. Effect on stability of motor vehicles
SIDEWINDS
Effects on stability of motor vehicles

1.3.3 Entries for string 3:
DEVELOPING COUNTRIES
Economic planning. Implications of social change
ECONOMIC PLANNING. Developing countries
Implications of social change
SOCIAL CHANGE. Developing countries
Implications for economic planning

1.3.4 Note the use of the upwards reading connective (coded $w) in strings 1 and 2. In string 1 it is used to bring 'students' into the display when 'Home environment' is in the lead, otherwise the entry would read:
HOME ENVIRONMENT. Students
Influence on academic achievement
It has a similar effect in string 2, avoiding the entries
WINDS. Motor vehicles
Sidewinds. Effects on stability
and
SIDEWINDS. Motor vehicles
Effects on stability

1.4 Format associated with operator (s)

1.4.1 General notes
A term coded (s) must always be 'fully gated', ie equipped with both upward and downward reading connectives; hence, it must also have both higher and lower terms even where these are only implied, eg

Subject Attitudes to death
String (2) dĕath
          (s) attitudes $v of $w to
          (3) society
Entries DEATH
            Attitudes of society
            ATTITUDES. Society
            To death

The term immediately below an (s) is always coded (3). This term plus its dependent elements, if any, will be referred to as 'the (3) block'.

1.4.2 When a term above the (s) is lead.
The entry format is governed by the role operator attached to the term in the lead.

1.4.3 When the term coded (s) is lead.
The (3) block is printed in Qualifier, terms being set down in the order in which they occur when reading up the block.

The upward reading connective attached to the term coded (s), plus the next higher term, plus terms linked to the next higher term by upward reading connectives, are printed in the Display.

Any higher terms in the string which have not been 'pulled down' into display complete the Qualifier. If there are any terms below the (3) block these complete the Display.

1.4.4 When a term within the (3) block is lead.
Higher terms in the block are printed in Qualifier. Lower terms are printed in Display, and are followed by the term coded (s) plus any higher terms linked to the (s) by upward reading connectives.

Any higher terms within the string which have not been 'pulled down' into display complete the Qualifier. If there are any terms below the (3) block, these complete the Display.

1.4.5 When a term below the (3) block is lead.
The entry format is governed by the role operator attached to the term in the lead.

1.4.6 Examples
    Subject The public accountability of industries for the pollution of
             the environment

77

String (1) environment
   (2) pollution $w of
   (s) accountability $i public $v of $w for
   (3) industries
Entries ENVIRONMENT
   Pollution. Public accountability of industries
   POLLUTION. Environment
   Public accountability of industries
   ACCOUNTABILITY. Industries
   Public accountability for pollution of environment
   PUBLIC ACCOUNTABILITY. Industries
   For pollution of environment
   INDUSTRIES
   Public accountability for pollution of environment
(3) block containing dependent elements.
 Subject The attitudes of girl students to teachers
 String (1) teachers
   (s) attitudes $v of $w to
   (3) students
   (q) girls
Entries TEACHERS
   Attitudes of students: Girls
   ATTITUDES. Girls. Students
   To teachers
   STUDENTS
   Girls. Attitudes to teachers
   GIRLS. Students
   Attitudes to teachers

2 *Author attributed association:* Operator (t)

2.1 We can divide action relationships into two categories:

2.1.1 system-initiated.
This is the normal type, introduced by operator (2), when the system (ie concept) named as agent is the one which is directly or indirectly responsible for a given action or effect. Thus 'Frost' may be said to initiate 'Damage' to 'Fruit trees'.

2.1.2 author attributed association.
This category assumes an observer, un-named in the string, who is

engaged in the literary task of relating together two or more concepts, or expounding one in terms of another.

2.2 The operator (t) is used for the second of the above categories. It triggers predicate transformation, and the words introduced by (t) are printed in italics. The terms immediately above and immediately below the term coded (t) are located as a special sequence and are printed in the entry as shown.

String (0) Victoria
          (1) high schools
          (t) compared with
          (1) technical schools
Entries VICTORIA
           High schools *compared with* technical schools
           HIGH SCHOOLS. Victoria
           compared with technical schools
           TECHNICAL SCHOOLS. Victoria
           compared with high schools

2.3 When the attributed association is two-way the terms linked will usually be introduced by the same operator, as in the above example. If, however, the relationship is one way, the agentive term will be coded (3).

String (1) Christianity
          (t) $v expounded by $w expounding
          (3) Marxism
Entries CHRISTIANITY
           expounded by Marxism
           MARXISM
           expounding Christianity

2.4 Coding terms linked to author attributed associations.

2.4.1 Coding terms linked to a two-way association.
The one or more terms above the (t) are coded in conventional manner. The term below the (t) may be:
   i) not related to any term above the (t)—in which case it will be coded (1) if an entity or (2) if an action.
or ii) related to a term above the (t)—in which case it will be coded according to its relationship with this term. For instance, in the

79

example below, since 'Intelligence' is logically a property of the higher term 'Students' it is coded (p).

    (1) universities
    (p) students
    (p) academic achievement
    (t) related to
    (p) intelligence

2.4.2 Coding terms linked to a one-way association.

The one or more terms above the (t) are coded in conventional manner. The term below the (t) is coded (3), since it has an agentive function.

    (1) nationalism
    (t) $v expounded by $w expounding
    (3) history

2.5 Non-standard formats: Format associated with operator (t).

2.5.1 General notes

One-way and two-way associations generate the same entry format. An author attributed association is never led. It is printed in italic without preceding or following punctuation. The term which follows it in an entry is printed with a lower case initial letter (unless it has been input with a capital initial).

For the purposes of the explanation below, a string is assumed to consist of:

  i) One or more terms above the sequence, eg (1) children
  ii) The *sequence:* a) the term above (t), eg   (p) intelligence
                     b) the term coded (t), eg   (t) related to
                     c) the term below (t), eg   (p) social class
  iii) One or more terms below the sequence, eg (2) research

2.5.2 When a term above the sequence is lead.

The sequence is read from top to bottom and printed in display:

        CHILDREN
             Intelligence *related to* social class. Research

2.5.3 When the first term in the sequence is lead.

The remainder of the sequence is read from top to bottom, and printed in display:

        INTELLIGENCE. Children
         related to social class. Research

2.5.4   When the last term in the sequence is lead.
The 'turntable effect' comes into operation, ie the form of entry is as for the predicate transformation:
> SOCIAL CLASS. Children
> *related to* intelligence. Research

2.5.5   When a term below the sequence is lead.
The sequence is read from bottom to top, and printed in an appropriate part of the entry:
> RESEARCH. Social class *related to* intelligence
> Children

2.5.6   Example
> *Subject*   A comparison of weather forecasting and astrology
> *String*   (1)   weather
> (2)   forecasting
> (sub 2) (2)   weather forecasting
> (t)   compared with
> (2)   astrology
> *Entries*   WEATHER
> Forecasting *compared with* astrology
> FORECASTING. Weather
> *compared with* astrology
> ASTROLOGY
> *compared with* weather forecasting

3.   *Checking exercise 7*
When you think you understand the material in this unit, work through the exercise which follows, and when you think you have arrived at a correct set of answers turn to the model answers at the back of the Workbook and compare them with your answers. If the model answer for any item differs from your solution, work through the item again to see where you went wrong.

Write PRECIS strings appropriate for the following items.   For example:
> *Item*   Participation by shop stewards in management in timber trades
> *String*   (1)   timber trades
> (2)   management
> (s)   participation $v by $w in
> (3)   shop stewards

81

1. Excavation of foundations for buildings in London
2. The effects of mass production on the reliability of cars
3. Empiricism and rationalism: a comparison
4. Application of queuing theory to the scheduling of bus services
5. Meaning explained in terms of information theory
6. Role of banks in housing finance
7. The role of game reserves in wildlife conservation
8. The application of computers in the control of space vehicles
9. British history expounded in English fiction (English fiction= Fiction in English)
10. Academic achievements related to social class in students in high schools in the United States

Write out the entries which would be produced by the following PRECIS strings.

11. (1) universities
    (p) students
    (p) academic achievement $w of
    (s) attitudes $v of $w to
    (3) academic personnel

12. (1) juveniles
    (2) crime
(sub 2) (2) juvenile crime
    (t) $v expounded by $w expounding
    (3) sociology

13. (1) industry
    (s) use $v of $w in
    (3) digital computers

14. (1) Australian rules football
    (t) compared with
    (1) soccer

15. (0) China
    (1) factory workers $w in
    (2) productivity $w of
    (s) effects $v of $w on
    (3) music $h background

82

UNIT 8

Coordinate concepts, theme interlinks and some indexing problems

1 Coordinate concepts: Operator (g)

1.1 The subjects considered so far have all been made up of concepts related in a strictly linear fashion, eg

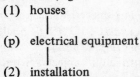

Some documents, however, deal with concepts which share a coordinate relationship with some other concepts, eg

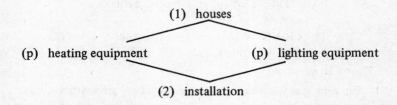

1.2 The two terms which share the coordinate relationship (in the above example *heating equipment* and *lighting equipment*) are referred to as the *coordinate* block. The relationship between the terms in the coordinate block is expressed by the operator (g), which is written in front of the second and any subsequent term, the first one being introduced by one of the main line or dependent codes. The penultimate term is accompanied by a conjunction (usually '&' or 'or') which is prefixed by the connective $v.

(1) hóuses
(p) héating equipment $v &
(g) lighting equipment
(2) installation

(1) schools
(p) cürriculum subjects
(q) músic
(g) póetry $v &
(g) páinting
(2) téaching

Entries from string 1.
> HOUSES
>> Heating equipment & lighting equipment. Installation
> HEATING EQUIPMENT. Houses
>> Installation
> LIGHTING EQUIPMENT. Houses
>> Installation
> INSTALLATION. Heating equipment & lighting equipment. Houses

Entries from string 2.
> SCHOOLS
>> Curriculum subjects: Music, poetry & painting. Teaching
> CURRICULUM SUBJECTS. Schools
>> Music, poetry & painting. Teaching
> MUSIC. Curriculum subjects. Schools
>> Teaching
> POETRY. Curriculum subjects. Schools
>> Teaching
> PAINTING. Curriculum subjects. Schools
>> Teaching
> TEACHING. Music, poetry & painting. Curriculum subjects. Schools

2 *Theme interlinks*

2.1 The principal function of these codes, which are written alongside and preceding main line and interposed operators, is to identify separate themes within a single string, eg if a document treated of both Heat insulation in schools & Water supply in hospitals, the content of the document may be set out in a single string:

first term in theme 1   (x) (1) schools
                        (y) (p) buildings (NU)
                        (y) (2) heat insulation
first term in theme 2   (x) (1) hóspitals
                        (y) (p) buildings (NU)
                        (y) (2) water supply services

Entries

Theme 1 {
SCHOOLS
    Buildings. Heat insulation
BUILDINGS. Schools
    Heat insulation
HEAT INSULATION. Schools

Theme 2 {
HOSPITALS
    Buildings. Water supply services
BUILDINGS. Hospitals
    Water supply services
WATER SUPPLY SERVICES. Hospitals

The operator (x) signifies the first term of a distinct theme and (y) the subsequent terms.

2.2 The operator (z) identifies concepts common to all themes of a document.

    Subject Heat insulation of school classrooms & hospital wards
    String

First term of theme 1	(x)	(1)	schools
	(y)	(p)	buildings (NU)
	(y)	(p)	classrooms
First term of theme 2	(x)	(1)	hospitals
	(y)	(p)	buildings (NU)
	(y)	(p)	wards
common term	(z)	(2)	heat insulation

Entries

Theme 1 {
SCHOOLS
    Buildings. Classrooms. Heat insulation
BUILDINGS. Schools
    Classrooms. Heat insulation
CLASSROOMS. Schools
    Heat insulation
HEAT INSULATION. Classrooms. Schools

Theme 2 {
HOSPITALS
    Buildings. Wards. Heat insulation
BUILDINGS. Hospitals
    Wards. Heat insulation
WARDS. Hospitals
    Heat insulation
HEAT INSULATION. Wards. Hospitals

85

2.3 Note that a string can never, in any circumstances, begin with (y). Strings which code one subject only, as is the case with the overwhelming majority of PRECIS strings, could be accompanied with the (z) interlink, since by definition all terms in the string are common terms—common to the one subject. For example:

      (z) (1) New Zealand
      (z) (2) foreign relations $v with $w with
      (z) (1) Japan

When strings are encoded for computer input the (z) interlink is, in fact, included, but for manual coding it is omitted and the string is written simply as:

      (1) New Zealand
      (2) foreign relations $v with $w with
      (1) Japan

3 Two-way interactions

3.1 It was noted above that action relationships are usually system-initiated. These are normally one-way, ie, they involve an agent and a system on which the action is performed. However, it is possible to identify also a category of *system initiated two-way interactions*. Subjects of this type lead to strings such as:

      (1) New Zealand
      (2) foreign relations $v with $w with
      (1) Japan

If the action is mutual and two way it will invariably be found that the same preposition has to be written twice. Note that the operator (1) appears *both above and below the action*. This (1) (2) (1) sequence triggers a special sequence of entries:

      NEW ZEALAND
          Foreign relations with Japan
      FOREIGN RELATIONS. New Zealand
          With Japan
      FOREIGN RELATIONS. Japan
          With New Zealand
      JAPAN
          Foreign relations with New Zealand

Note:

i) Predicate transformation in the fourth entry

ii) Double entry under the action term, a different entity appearing in the qualifier position in each case.

86

4 *Directional properties*

4.1 A document which *presents* the viewpoint of a group of people will call for the operator (4)—see Unit 5. Such a document should be distinguished from one which *discusses* the attitudes of a group of people.

4.2 Attitudes regarded as a general phenomenon (ie, neither the holder nor the object is specifically named) would be coded simply as:
>   (1) attitudes

4.3 If the attitudes of an identified class of person is the subject being indexed then 'attitudes' is regarded as a software component and coded (p):
>   (1) students
>   (p) attitudes

4.4 The situation becomes more complex when the author discusses the attitudes of a group of people towards a named thing or event, eg, 'The attitude of university students towards the curriculum'. This situation calls for use of the operator (s):
>   (1) universities
>   (p) curriculum
>   (s) attitudes $v of $w to
>   (3) students
>   UNIVERSITIES
>   Curriculum. Attitudes of students
>   CURRICULUM. Universities
>   Attitudes of students
>   ATTITUDES. Students. Universities
>   To curriculum
>   STUDENTS. Universities
>   Attitudes to curriculum

4.5 There is a special condition attached to the use of the operator (s) which must be remembered: it must always be accompanied by both a higher and a lower term. This means that we cannot express the attitude and the object of the attitude without also expressing the holder. For example, a general work on attitudes to women cannot be indexed as:

(1) wómen
(s) attitudes $w to

This string is invalid because there is no lower term to accompany the operator (s).

4.6 The problem cannot be solved by the use of the operator (2), because the entries from a string:
(1) wómen
(2) attitudes $w to

would be indistinguishable from the entries for a document on the attitudes of women:
(1) wómen
(p) attitudes

4.7 It follows that the holder of the attitudes must be included in the string, even if only in general terms, ie, Attitudes to women calls for the string:
(1) wómen
(2) attitudes $v of $w to
(3) sóciety

This string would produce the entries:

WOMEN
    Attitudes of society
ATTITUDES. Society
    To women
SOCIETY
    Attitudes to women

5 *Compound agent*

5.1 If we consider 'Pollution of the atmosphere' and 'Diseases of the respiratory system' as separate subjects they produce the following strings and entries.

String   (1) atmosphere
          (2) póllution
Entries ATMOSPHERE
           Pollution
          POLLUTION. Atmosphere
String   (1) respiratory system
          (2) diseases

Entries RESPIRATORY SYSTEM
 Diseases
 DISEASES. Respiratory system

5.2 If we have to write a string for a complex subject comprising these two themes we must achieve collocation with these entries. Such a subject might be, for example 'The effect of pollution of the atmosphere on diseases of the respiratory system'.

5.3 It is not possible to express this subject as a single theme and produce satisfactory entries. It is necessary to express the subject as two separate themes using the theme interlinks (x) and (y).
 String (x) (1) rĕspiratory system
  (y) (2) diseases
  (y) (2) effects of atmospheric pollution
  (x) (1) aťmosphere
  (y) (2) póllution
  (y) (2) effects on respiratory disease
 Entries RESPIRATORY SYSTEM
  Diseases. Effects of atmospheric pollution
  DISEASES. Respiratory system
  Effects of atmospheric pollution
  ATMOSPHERE
  Pollution. Effects on respiratory diseases
  POLLUTION. Atmosphere
  Effects on respiratory diseases
'Effects' is here coded (2) because there is no lower term in the string.

6 *Checking exercise 8*
When you think you understand the material in this unit, work through the exercise which follows, and when you think you have arrived at a correct set of answers turn to the model answers at the back of the Workbook and compare them with your answers. If the model answer for any item differs from your solution, work through the item again to see where you went wrong.
 Write PRECIS strings appropriate for the following items. For example:
 Item Foreign relations of India and China
 String (1) Iňdia
  (2) fóreign relations $v with $w with
  (1) Cȟina

89

1. Chile's frontier disputes with Peru
2. Cooperation between libraries and museums
3. The storage of apples and pears in Italy
4. The cataloguing of cinema films, slides and filmstrips in libraries
5. The relationship between prices and incomes
6. The harvesting of apples, and the storage of pears, in Italy
7. The relationship between profits and wages on the one hand, and inflation on the other, in Japan
8. Colonisation by France in the Pacific Region
9. The sales of Australian films and television programmes in Great Britain
10. The relationship between the use of seat belts in cars and the reduction in road accident deaths in Canada.

Write out the entries which would be produced by the following PRECIS strings.

11. (1) children
    (s) attitudes $v of $w to
    (3) old people

12. (0) France
    (1) mental hospitals
    (p) personnel (NU)
    (q) nurses
    (2) absenteeism $v&
    (g) sickness

13. (z) (0) Australia
    (z) (1) television industry
    (x) (p) film scripts
    (y) (2) writing
    (x) (2) advertising
    (y) (2) administration

14. (1) navigational aids
    (s) use $v by $w of
    (3) ships
    (g) submarines $v&
    (g) aircraft

15. (1) United States
    (2) trade $v with $w with
    (1) China

PART II

THE SEMANTIC PART OF PRECIS

UNIT 9

1 In an alphabetical subject indexing system there are two kinds of references.

2. 'See' references deal with what are sometimes called *equivalence* relationships. They are concerned with vocabulary control. In an alphabetical subject indexing system it is most important that any given concept be named consistently, ie, that the same word or words be used to name it. For example we must consistently use either 'Cars' or 'Motor cars' or 'Automobiles', otherwise entries for the same concept will be scattered. Whichever term we adopt as the entry term we must provide references from the rejected terms so that a user, looking in the index under a rejected term, will be guided to the correct term. Thus, if 'cars' is adopted as the entry term we must provide the references:

Automobiles   *See* CARS
Motor cars   *See* CARS

2.1 This is principally a question of controlling the use of synonyms, as in the example above.

2.2 We should refer also from unused antonyms. For example, a document on Temperance is also about Intemperance: if one advocates temperance one also necessarily condemns intemperance. We usually prefer the more 'positive' antonym. Thus

Intemperance *See* TEMPERANCE

2.3 It is a convention in indexing that we use the plural form of a noun for things which are countable. Occasionally we should refer from the singular form of a noun, eg,

92

Cat   *See* CATS

This is necessary when the two forms of the noun may be separated. Many terms may file between 'Cat' and 'Cats', eg, catacombs, catalogues, catalysts, catamarans, catapults, cataracts, etc.

3. 'See also' references are used to deal with subject relationships. They link terms which name related subjects. The network of 'see also' references in an alphabetical subject catalogue is known as the *syndetic structure*.

3.1 The hierarchical subject relationship covers two types of relationships.

3.1.1 The *true generic* relationship is that of class inclusion, ie, the relationship between a genus and its species.

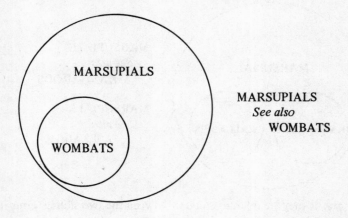

MARSUPIALS
See also
     WOMBATS

The relationship may also be displayed in a 'tree' diagram

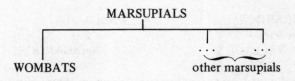

It is important that these references should be proximate, ie, the references should proceed one step at a time.

93

ANIMALS		VERTEBRATES
See also	and	*See also*
VERTEBRATES		REPTILES

not   ANIMALS
                             See also
                             REPTILES

3.1.2 Hierarchical *whole-part* relationships include
   a)   geographical regions, eg, Nova Scotia is part of Canada;
   b)   systems and organs of the body, eg, the heart is part of the
cardiovascular system; and
   c)   areas of discourse (or disciplines), eg, Botany is part of Biology

3.2 Sibling relationships occur when two terms bear the same relationship with a common higher term

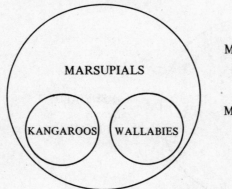

MARSUPIALS
See also
   KANGAROOS

MARSUPIALS
See also
   WALLABIES

In this case it may be relevant to refer between the two sibling terms if
the relationship is significant. For example, it would probably be relevant to refer between 'Kitchens' and 'Dining rooms' but not between
'Kitchens' and 'Bedrooms'. So the relationship illustrated above would
yield:

KANGAROOS	WALLABIES
See also	*See also*
WALLABIES	KANGAROOS

3.3 Finally we have the *associative*, or cross-category, relationship, ie,
the two terms are mentally associated without being part of the same
hierarchy. This usually involves a defining or explaining role, for

example 'Feet' and 'Chiropody' are linked associatively because the concept of 'Feet' is an integral part of the definition of 'Chiropody'. The reference is always made *towards* the term which helps to explain the other, eg,

CHIROPODY
> *See also*
>> FEET

A reciprocal reference (ie, *from* the term which helps to explain the other) may be made if required, eg,

FEET
> *See also*
>> CHIROPODY

4 After a PRECIS string has been written each term which has been marked as a lead is considered. If any term has not previously been used in PRECIS, equivalent terms, such as synonyms, and hierarchical, sibling and associative terms, are determined by checking classification schemes, thesauri and dictionaries. In this way a network of references is created. Webster's *Third international dictionary* has been found to be a particularly valuable tool for this purpose.

5 Suppose, for example, that the term 'Toes' is admitted to the system. A hierarchically related term is 'Feet' (Toes are a part of Feet). We now consider this term and we find that an equivalence relationship should be recognised with the singular form of the noun—Foot—which will file quite separately (see para 2.3 above). We may recognise 'Ankles' as a relevant sibling term and Chiropody as an associative term; the higher term is Limbs.

5.1 In this way we establish the pattern of relationships shown diagramatically below.

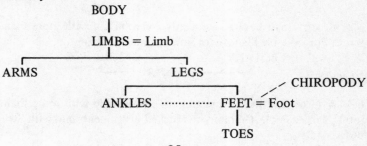

95

An equals sign indicates an equivalent relationship.
A continuous line indicates a hierarchical relationship.
A dotted line indicates a significant sibling relationship.
A dashed line indicates an associative relationship.

5.2   The references would be as follows.

BODY	Limb *See* LIMBS
See also	
LIMBS	

LIMBS	LIMBS
See also	*See also*
ARMS	LEGS
LEGS	LEGS
See also	*See also*
ANKLES	FEET
ANKLES	FEET
See also	*See also*
FEET	ANKLES
CHIROPODY	FEET
See also	*See also*
FEET	CHIROPODY
Foot *see* FEET	FEET
	See also
	TOES

6   It is possible for a term to have the same relationship with more than one term.

6.1   A term may have an equivalent relationship with more than one term. For example, Temperance with Intemperance and Teetotalism.
Intemperance = TEMPERANCE = Teetotalism

6.2   A term may have an associative relationship with more than one term. For example Plants with Botany and Gardening

BOTANY   GARDENING
└─────── PLANTS ───────┘

6.3   A term may have a hierarchical relationship with more than one term. For example, Guitars with Plucked instruments and with Stringed instruments.

```
           ┌──── MUSICAL INSTRUMENTS ────┐
 PLUCKED INSTRUMENTS      STRINGED INSTRUMENTS
           └──────── GUITARS ────────┘
```

7 Checking exercise 9

When you think you understand the material in this unit, work through
the exercise which follows, and when you think you have arrived at a
correct solution turn to the model answers at the back of the Workbook and compare your solution. If there are any discrepancies between
your answer and the model answer check to see where you went
wrong.

Using only the terms listed below draw up a semantic network similar
to the one shown in para 5.1 above.

Animals	Koalas*	Reptiles
Aquatic birds	Living systems	Sea birds
Aves	Mammals	Sphenisciforms
Biology	Marine birds	Veterinary Science
Birds	Nocturnal animals	Wallabies
Fauna	Ornithology	Water birds
Kangaroos	Penguins	Zoology
		Marsupials

*Koalas are nocturnal marsupials

UNIT 10

Coding references
1   As we noted in Unit 9, if any term in a PRECIS string has not previously been used it is examined and its relationships with other terms
are established.

2   A special 'Reference Indicator Number' (RIN) is assigned to each
term not previously admitted to the system (ie, not previously used).
This RIN indicates the position in the machine-readable authority file,
or thesaurus, (in computer parlance the "address") at which the following data are held:
   a)   the term being admitted;
   b)   codes which identify the kinds of reference which should be
   made towards this term; and
   c)   the addresses of the terms from which references should be
   made.

3   The codes identifying the kinds of reference are as follows:
   $m   Make a 'see' reference from the term at the address which
          follows
          Make a 'see also' reference from the term at the address which
          follows
   $n   Term in a different category; no reciprocal reference is required
   $o   Term is a higher term in the same hierarchy
   $x   Term is a sibling
   $y   Term is a different category; reciprocal reference is required

4   The information noted in para 2 above is recorded on a form ready
for computer input.   For example

PENGUINS	SPHENISCIFORMS	BIRDS
000 506 222	$m 000 506 230	$o 000 400 254

5   This signifies that 'Penguins' has been admitted as a term and assigned the RIN 000 506 222. A 'see' reference will be generated from 'Sphenisciforms' and a 'see also' reference from 'Birds'.

6   Each of the terms from which a reference is generated is recorded and allocated a RIN. Any term from which a 'see also' reference was requested is then considered in its turn and any necessary references established. The information is again recorded. For example

BIRDS 000 400 254	AVES $m 000 400 246	VERTEBRATES $o 000 204 17X
	ORNITHOLOGY $n 000 902 083	

7   The operation is then repeated for terms on this record from which a 'see also' reference is required.

8   In the examples discussed so far in this unit, the 'see also' references are in one direction only, eg,

BIRDS		PENGUINS
See also	but not	*See also*
PENGUINS		BIRDS

There are, however, situations in which a reference is required in both directions.

8.1   For example

EMPLOYMENT

CONDITIONS OF SERVICE   WORKING CONDITIONS

In this case it would be appropriate to make the reciprocal references:

CONDITIONS OF SERVICE		WORKING CONDITIONS
See also	and	*See also*
WORKING CONDITIONS		CONDITIONS OF SERVICE

as well as the two references from the higher term:

EMPLOYMENT		EMPLOYMENT
See also	and	*See also*
CONDITIONS OF SERVICE		WORKING CONDITIONS

8.2   However, if we used the code $o or $n to generate the references between 'Conditions of service' and 'Working conditions' the computer would oscillate between these sibling terms. Quoting the RIN for 'Conditions of service' would send the computer to the address (RIN) for 'Employment' to create the reference:

EMPLOYMENT
   See also
   CONDITIONS OF SERVICE

and to the address of 'Working conditions' to create the reference

WORKING CONDITIONS
   See also
   CONDITIONS OF SERVICE

8.3 At the RIN for 'Working conditions' it finds an instruction directing it to 'Employment' to create a reference

EMPLOYMENT
   See also
   WORKING CONDITIONS

and to the address for 'Conditions of employment' to create the reference

CONDITIONS OF SERVICE
   See also
   WORKING CONDITIONS

8.4 At the RIN for 'Conditions of employment' the computer finds instructions directing it to the RIN for 'Employment' and to the RIN for 'Working conditions' and the cycle begins all over again.

8.5 This looping is avoided by using a special code: $x.

9 The records for these three terms would, therefore, be as follows:

EMPLOYMENT		
001 706 020		

CONDITIONS OF SERVICE	EMPLOYMENT	WORKING CONDITIONS
005 505 054	$o 001 706 020	$x 019 509 057

WORKING CONDITIONS	EMPLOYMENT	CONDITIONS OF SERVICE
019 509 057	$o 001 706 020	$x 005 505 054

10 The $x convention is used when the linked terms are siblings. However, exactly the same problem may occur if it is desired to make reciprocal references between terms in different hierarchies. For example

100

ZOOLOGY   ANIMALS
   See also   *See also*
      ANIMALS   ZOOLOGY

In this case the special code $y is used.

ANIMALS	FAUNA	ZOOLOGY
000 100 218	$m 005 600 022	$y 000 100 234

ZOOLOGY	BIOLOGY	ANIMALS
000 100 234	$o 000 100 242	$y 000 100 218

11   The instructions built into the codes $x and $y are as follows:

a)   Proceed to the indicated address (eg, 000 100 218)

b)   Construct a 'see also' reference from the term at that address to the target term, eg,

   ANIMALS
     See also
       ZOOLOGY

c)   Ignore all other relational codes at the new address except $m. Thus being sent to 000 100 218 the machine will construct the reference

   FAUNA *see* ANIMALS

but not a 'see also' reference from ZOOLOGY.

12 *Polyhierarchical relationships*

12.1 In the examples shown so far only one example of each relational code appears on the record for any one target term. However, as we noted in the previous unit, a term may have the same relationship with more than one other term. The codes $m, $n and $o may, therefore, occur more than once at the same address, indicating that the target term shares an equivalent relationship, an associative relationship, or a hierarchical relationship with more than one other term.

12.2 We noted, for example, that Guitars reflects the following hierarchy.

              MUSICAL INSTRUMENTS

PLUCKED INSTRUMENTS   STRINGED INSTRUMENTS

                 GUITARS

12.3   The following records would be made

MUSICAL INSTRUMENTS
000 402 170

PLUCKED INSTRUMENTS
000 402 095

MUSICAL INSTRUMENTS
$o 000 402 170

STRINGED INSTRUMENTS
000 402 060

MUSICAL INSTRUMENTS
$o 000 402 170

GUITARS   STRINGED INSTRUMENTS   PLUCKED INSTRUMENTS
000 402 087 $o 000 402 060 $o 000 402 095

12.4   The following references would be generated

MUSICAL INSTRUMENTS
   See also
      PLUCKED INSTRUMENTS
PLUCKED INSTRUMENTS
   See also
      GUITARS

MUSICAL INSTRUMENTS
   See also
      STRINGED INSTRUMENTS
STRINGED INSTRUMENTS
   See also
      GUITARS

13   *Checking exercise 10*

When you think you understand the material in this unit, work through the exercise which follows, and when you think you have arrived at a correct solution turn to the model answer at the back of the Workbook and compare it with your solution. If there are any discrepancies between your answer and the model answer check to see where you went wrong.

1   Write out the records which would be required for the following terms

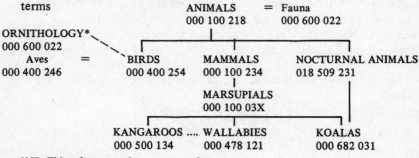

ANIMALS   = Fauna
000 100 218   000 600 022

ORNITHOLOGY*
000 600 022
   Aves   =   BIRDS   MAMMALS   NOCTURNAL ANIMALS
000 400 246   000 400 254   000 100 234   018 509 231

MARSUPIALS
000 100 03X

KANGAROOS .... WALLABIES   KOALAS
000 500 134   000 478 121   000 682 031

*NB This reference to be one-way only.

102

2. Write out the references which would be produced by the following records

2.1
| GRANITE | IGNEOUS ROCKS | ACIDIC ROCKS |
| 018 508 022 | $o 018 508 014 | $o 018 601 251 |

2.2
| GULLS | LARIDAE | MARINE BIRDS |
| 002 804 158 | $m 007 904 231 | $o 018 508 138 |

2.3
| SRI LANKA | SOUTH ASIA | CEYLON |
| 007 300 174 | $o 004 204 115 | $m 018 601 022 |

2.4
| LIGHT | ENERGY | OPTICS |
| 008 206 023 | $o 007 509 253 | $y 002 900 084 |

2.5
| VENTILATION | AIR CONDITIONING |
| 018 903 045 | $x 018 903 061 |

2.6
| SKULLS | ETHNOLOGY |
| 008 107 22X | $n 000 206 202 |

PART III

MANIPULATION CODES

UNIT 11

Computer manipulation codes

1 The instructions to the computer as to how to manipulate the terms
in the concept string, indicated so far by the codes and conventions (eg
√, NU), are encoded in a machine-intelligible manipulation string.
These strings may appear daunting to the uninitiated, but they merely
code the decisions which you have learned to make in the foregoing
parts of this manual, and the difficulties which you might encounter in
learning this system from scratch have already been anticipated.

2 The manipulation string consists of a series of alpha-numeric
characters, with $ acting as a sub-field indicator.
Example

The indexer writes:	(1)	rǎilways
	(p)	brǐdges $i concrete
	(2)	maintenance
This is encoded:		$z11030$arailways
		$zp1030$abridges$iconcrete
		$z20030$amaintenance

3 The manipulation string, then, is the means by which indexing decisions regarding the appearance of the entry, eg the appearance or non-
appearance of a term in the lead, qualifier or display positions, are
conveyed to the computer.

4. There are nine positions in the manipulation string.

1	2	3	4	5	6	7	8	9
$	z	1	1	0	3	0	$	a

4.1 Position 1. Sub-field indicator. Indicates to the computer that
what follow are codes and not indexing terms.

4.2 Position 2. Theme inter-link. May be x, y or z (see unit on theme inter-links).

4.3 Position 3. Role operator.

4.4 Position 4. Lead or non-lead   1 = lead, 0 = non-lead   (ie 1 is equivalent to √).

4.5 Position 5. Substitution. 0 indicates no substitution, ie the terms which follow are not a substitute phrase. 1-9 indicates substitution, ie, the term(s) which follow are a substitute phrase and the number used (1-9) indicates the number of higher terms for which the encoded term is to be substituted. Thus 2 in position 5 is equivalent to writing (sub 2).

4.6 Position 6. Indicates whether a term is required in qualifier or display.

Qualifier	Display	Code	Equivalent
Yes	Yes	3	
Yes	No	2	(ND)
No	Yes	1	(NU)
No	No	0	(LO)

4.7 Position 7. Position unused; always 0.

4.8 Position 8. Sub-field indicator. Indicates that after next character the manipulation codes will end.

4.9 Position 9. Indicates type of term. Usually a, but a "class of one" should be coded c.

5 *Examples*

5.1

    String (0) United States
             (1) rǎilways
             (p) lócomotives
             (2) maintenance

Input to computer
\$z00030\$aUnited States\$z11030\$arailways\$zp1030\$alocomotives
\$z20030\$amaintenance

107

Entries   RAILWAYS. United States
            Locomotives. Maintenance
         LOCOMOTIVES. Railways. United States
            Maintenance

5.2
   String   (0) France
             (1) cathedrals (NU)
             (q) Chartres Cathedral
             (p) windows
             (p) stained glass

Input to computer
$z01030$aFrance$z11010$acathedrals$zq1030$cChartres Cathedral
$z1030$awindows$zp1030$astained glass

   Entries   FRANCE
               Cathedrals: Chartres Cathedral. Windows. Stained glass
            CATHEDRALS. France
               Chartres Cathedral. Windows. Stained glass
            CHARTRES CATHEDRAL. France
               Windows. Stained glass
            WINDOWS. Chartres Cathedral. France
               Stained glass
            STAINED GLASS. Windows. Chartres Cathedral. France

5.3
   String   (2) medicine
               (p) research
      (sub 2) (2) medical research
               (2) planning

Input to computer
$z21030$amedicine$zp0030$aresearch$z20220$amedical research
$z21030$aplanning

   Entries   MEDICINE
               Research. Planning
            PLANNING. Medical research

5.4
   String   (z) (1) lubricating oils
             (x) (p) contaminants $w of
             (y) (q) water
             (x) (p) viscosity
             (y) (2) measurement

108

Input to computer.
$z11030$alubricating oils$xp1030$acontaminantswofyq1030
$awater$xp1030$aviscosity$y20030$ameasurement

   Entries LUBRICATING OILS
           Contaminants: Water
         CONTAMINANTS. Lubricating oils
           Water
         WATER. Contaminants of lubricating oils
         LUBRICATING OILS
           Viscosity. Measurement
         VISCOSITY. Lubricating oils
           Measurement

6 Note that differences and/or connectives are written as in the concept string, but without any spacing, eg

        (1) bridges $i concrete $ m reinforced
        $z11030$abridges$iconcrete$mreinforced

        (1) houses
        (2) damage $v by $w to
        (3) winds
$z11030$ahouses$z21030damage$vbywtoz31030$awinds

7 *Checking exercise 11*

When you think you understand the material in this unit, work through the exercise which follows and when you have arrived at what you believe to be a correct set of answers turn to the model answers at the back of the Workbook and compare them with your answers. If the model answer for any item differs from your solution work through the item again to see where you went wrong.

    Write out the computer input for each of the following concept strings. For example:

   String (1) cars
         (p) doors
         (p) hinges

Input
$z11030$acars$zp1030$adoors$zp1030$ahinges

1. (0) Italy   2. (0) Australia
     (1) natural resources   (1) migrants
     (q) rivers   (2) education

3. (1) vertebrates
   (p) anatomy
   (5) study examples
   (q) dogfish

4. (0) Bohemia
   (1) glassware
   (q) bowls $i decorative
   (2) manufacture

5. (0) Victoria
   (1) cables $i electrical $k high voltage $i insulated $m plastic
   (2) manufacture

6. (1) crops
   (2) damage $v by $w of
   (3) frost

7. (1) schools
   (2) administration
   (s) role $v of $w in
   (3) teachers

8. (1) hippies
   (r) communes
   (sub 2) (1) hippie communes
   (p) social structure

9. (x) (1) schools
   (y) (p) buildings (NU)
   (y) (2) heat insulation
   (x) (1) hospitals
   (y) (p) buildings (NU)
   (y) (p) water supply
            services

10. (1) rural regions
    (2) economic development $w of
    (s) role $v of $w in
    (3) social scientists
    (sub 4) (2) role of social scientists in economic development of rural
            regions
    (2) research

PART IV

PRESENT AND FUTURE

UNIT 12

Applications

Apart from its use in BNB and ANB, PRECIS is used in a number of libraries in Britain, for example the Sheffield College of Education and the Polytechnic of Central London. It is also used in bibliographies other than the two previously mentioned, for example the *British national film catalogue* and the *Film catalogue* of the College Bibliocentre at Don Mills, Ontario, in Canada. The National Film Board of Canada has recently completed production of a PRECIS index to the printed catalogue of its products and the system is being applied experimentally to the national map collection of Archive Canada in Ottowa.

It has been found that PRECIS works successfully with languages other than English, and some examples of foreign language entries follow. This opens up interesting possibilities, especially for countries with bi-lingual communities. It is possible to envisage a sequence of operations whereby an indexer, working, say, in English, produces a string:

    (1)   aircraft
    (2)   landing
    (s)   awareness $v of $w during
    (3)   crews

These components would then be checked against a thesaurus which contains not only the substantive terms but also all the supporting data, eg the codes $v and $w plus their prepositions. A new string is then produced, consisting of role operators plus RINS, eg

    (1)   001 401 05X
    (2)   005 704 073
    (s)   000 409 12X
    (3)   000 202 177

The computer then checks this string against a reconciled thesaurus in English and French and produces the following two sets of index entries plus the necessary references.

AIRCRAFT
   Landing. Awareness of crews
LANDING. Aircraft
   Awareness of crews
AWARENESS. Crews. Aircraft
   During landing
CREWS. Aircraft
   Awareness during landing
AVIONS
   Atterrissage. Perceptions conscientes des équipages
ATTERRISSAGE. Avions
   Perceptions conscientes des équipages
PERCEPTIONS CONSCIENTES. Equipages. Avions
   Pendant l'atterrissage
EQUIPAGES. Avions
   Perceptions conscientes pendant l'atterrissage

Examples of foreign language entries
a) *French*
English string and entries:
   (1) rǎilways
   (p) brǐdges $i foot $i concrete $m reinforced
        $k lightweight
RAILWAYS
   Lightweight reinforced concrete foot bridges
BRIDGES. Railways
   Lightweight reinforced concrete foot bridges
FOOT BRIDGES. Railways
   Lightweight reinforced concrete foot bridges
CONCRETE BRIDGES. Railways
   Lightweight reinforced concrete foot bridges
REINFORCED CONCRETE BRIDGES. Railways
   Lightweight reinforced concrete foot bridges
French string and entries:
   (1) chěmins de fer
   (p) běton armé léger $i passerelles en
CHEMINS DE FER
   Passarelles en béton armé léger
BETON ARME LEGER. Chemins de fer
   Passarelles en béton armé léger

113

PASSERELLES EN BETON ARME LEGER. Chemins de fer
PONTS
Voir aussi
PASSERELLES

b) *German*
English string and entries:
        (1) úrban regions
        (2) régional planning
(sub 2) (2) urbån planning
        (s) role $v of $w in
        (3) sócial scientists
URBAN REGIONS
    Regional planning. Role of social scientists
REGIONAL PLANNING. Urban regions
    Role of social scientists
SOCIAL SCIENTISTS
    Role in urban planning
German string and entries:
        (1) Stadgebiete
        (2) Régionplanung
(sub 2) (2) städtischer Planung
        (s) Rolle $v von $w in
        (3) Sozialwissenschlafter $1 Sozialwissenschlaftern
STADGEBIETE
    Regionplanung. Rolle von Sozialwissenschlaftern
REGIONPLANUNG
    Rolle von Sozialwissenschlaftern
SOZIALWISSENSCHLAFTER
    Rolle in städtischer Planung

NB: $1 is a special operator for foreign languages to cope with changes in word endings

c) *Dutch*
English string and entries:
        (1) urban regions
        (2) régional planning
(sub 2) (2) urban planning
        (s) role $v of $w in
        (3) sócial scientists

URBAN REGIONS
Regional planning. Role of social scientists
REGIONAL PLANNING. Urban regions
Role of social scientists
SOCIAL SCIENTISTS
Role in urban planning

Dutch string and entries:
- (1) st̆edelijke agglomeraties
- (2) r̆egionale planning
- (sub 2) (2) stedebouwkunde
- (s) fŭnctie $v van $w in de
- (3) sŏciologen

STEDELIJKE AGGLOMERATIES
Regionale planning. Functie van sociologen
REGIONALE PLANNING. Stedelijke agglomeraties
Functie van sociologen
SOCIOLOGEN
Functie in de stedbouwkunde

d) *Spanish*

English string and entries:
- (1) ŭrban regions
- (2) r̆egional planning
- (sub 2) (2) urban planning
- (s) role $v of $w in
- (3) sŏcial scientists

URBAN REGIONS
Regional planning. Role of social scientists
REGIONAL PLANNING. Urban regions
Role of social scientists
SOCIAL SCIENTISTS
Role in urban planning

Spanish string and entries:
- (1) r̆egiones urbanas
- (2) planificación regional
- (sub 2) (2) urbanisims
- (s) función $v de los $w en
- (3) sociólogos

REGIONES URBANAS
Planificación regional. Función de los sociólogos

PLANIFICACION REGIONAL. Regiones urbanas
    Función de los sociólogos
SOCIOLOGOS
    Función en urbanisims

e) *Finnish*

English string and entries:

       (1) úrban regions
       (2) régional planning
(sub 2) (2) urban planning
       (s) role $v of $w in
       (3) sócial scientists
URBAN REGIONS
    Regional planning. Role of social scientists
REGIONAL PLANNING. Urban regions
    Role of social scientists
SOCIAL SCIENTISTS
    Role in urban planning

Finnish string and entries:

   (x) (1) káupunkilaisseutuja
   (y) (2) séutukuntasuunitelma
   (y) (3) sosiologein rooli
   (x) (1) sósiologeja
   (y) (p) rooli kaupunkilaissuunitelmassa
KAUPUNKILAISSEUTUJA
    Sentukurtasuunitelma. Sosiologein rooli
SEUTUKUNTASUUNITELMA. Kaupunkilaisseutuja
    Sosiologein rooli
SOSIOLOGEJA
    Rooli kaupunkilaissuunitelmassa

One problem in developing an entirely successful means of switching from any one language into any other, using PRECIS, arises from the different ways in which grammatical functions (or roles) are expressed in different language systems. From the point of view of PRECIS, languages may be said to fall into one of two groups:

a) those which employ a wide range of prepositions to express grammatical role, with or without inflection;

b) those which have only a limited range of prepositions, grammatical role being expressed by means of adjectival phrases, whether or not inflections are used as well.

116

The pattern of operators used for (a) is different from that used for (b), but there appears to be consistency within the two groups.

French, German, Dutch and Spanish belong to the first group. Finnish belongs to the second group.

Checking exercise 12

The questions below are not related to the material in this unit but are designed rather to assist you in revision of material presented in Units 1-8. Model answers are provided at the back of the Workbook.

Write PRECIS strings appropriate for the following items.
1. The design of natural gas pipelines in Europe
2. The preservation of Anglo-Saxon illuminated manuscripts
3. An inquiry report into aboriginal land rights in Australia
4. The strike by air traffic controllers in Australia, 1977
5. The influence of television on the reading of children
6. Typing as a subject in British secondary schools
7. Attitudes to war in France
8. The extension of runways, taxiways and aviation aprons at London's Heathrow Airport
9. A catalogue of the paintings in the Wallace Collection in London
10. The secretion of steroid hormones by the endocrine system in mammals

Now write out the entries which would be produced by the following PRECIS strings.

11. (1) motor car industry
    (2) advertising
    (t) related to
    (2) sales

12. (0) Victoria
    (1) birds $i water
    (6) field guides

13. (0) Melbourne
    (1) airports (NU)
    (q) Tullamarine Airport
    (p) winds
    (p) velocity
    (2) measurement

14. (1) turtles
    (2) ecology
    (5) study regions
    (q) Great Barrier Reef

117

15. (z) (0) Nórthern Territory
    (z) (p) Aŕnhem Land
    (x) (1) róck carvings $i aboriginal
    (y) (2) pŕeservation
    (x) (1) bárk painting $i aboriginal
    (y) (2) collection

Further reading

The authoritative and detailed manual on the system is:

AUSTIN, Derek. *PRECIS: a manual of concept indexing.* London: BNB, 1973. (ISBN: 0 900220 42 2)

A primer is also being compiled for those who prefer a less detailed guide:

AUSTIN, Derek and DYKSTRA, Mary. *PRECIS primer.* (To be published jointly by Dalhousie University and BNB).

A key article is:

AUSTIN, Derek. 'The development of PRECIS: a theoretical and technical history' in *Journal of documentation*, v.30 no. 1 (March, 1974) p. 47-102.

MODEL ANSWERS

Checking exercise 1
Answers

1   CAT
        Dog. Hen. Pig
      DOG. Cat
        Hen. Pig
      HEN. Dog. Cat
        Pig
      PIG. Hen. Dog. Cat
In this example each term was ticked and therefore takes its turn in the
lead position in the standard shunting procedure. See Section 2.2.

2   DOG. Cat
        Hen. Pig
      HEN. Dog. Cat
        Pig
In this example 'Cat' and 'pig' were not ticked, and thus no entry is
made under these terms, ie they do not appear in the lead position. See
Section 4.1.

3   CAT
        Dog. Hen. Pig
      DOG. Cat
        Hen. Pig
      PIG. Hen. Cat
In this example 'Hen' was not ticked and therefore does not appear in
the lead position. In addition 'Dog' was marked (NU) and so does not
appear in the qualifier position. See Sections 4.1 and 4.3.

4   CAT
        Hen. Pig
      DOG. Cat
        Hen. Pig
      PIG. Hen. Dog. Cat
Once again 'Hen' was not ticked and therefore does not appear in the
lead. This time, in addition, 'Dog' was marked (ND) and so does not
appear in the display position. See Sections 4.1 and 4.3.

5   CAT
        Hen. Pig
    DOG. Cat
        Hen. Pig
    PIG. Hen. Cat

As in the two previous examples 'Hen' was not ticked. This time 'Dog' was marked (LO) and so does not appear in *either* the qualifier *or* the display position; it prints only in the lead. See Section 4.2.

6   CAT
        Dog. Hen. Pig
    HEN. Dog. Cat
        Pig
    PIG. Hen of dog. Cat

This item illustrates the upwards reading connective. The term 'Hen' is gated, ie it has an accompanying connective. On this occasion the connective is coded $w, ie it is an upwards reading connective, to be read when the string is read upwards (Pig, Hen of dog, Cat). Thus the connective is printed when 'Hen' is in the qualifier position. See Section 4.5.

7   CAT
        Dog. Hen by pig
    HEN. Dog. Cat
        By pig
    PIG. Hen. Dog. Cat

This item illustrates the downwards reading connective. The term 'Hen' is gated, ie it has an accompanying connective. On this occasion the connective is coded $v, ie it is a downwards reading connective, to be read when the string is read downwards (Cat, Dog, Hen by pig). Thus the connective prints in the display position until 'Hen' has passed into the qualifier position. See Section 4.6.

8   CAT
        Dog. Hen by pig
    HEN. Dog. Cat
        By pig
    PIG. Hen of dog. Cat

In this example 'Hen' is fully gated, ie it has both upwards and downwards connectives. The text for item 6 explains the upwards reading connective ($w) and the text for item 7 explains the downwards reading connective ($v). See Section 4.6.

9   CAT
         Dog. Hen by pig
     DOG. Cat
         Hen by pig
     HEN. Dog on cat
         By pig
     PIG. Hen of dog on cat

The upwards reading connective ('on') attached to 'Dog' is printed when 'Dog' is in the qualifier position, and when 'Hen' is in the qualifier position its upwards reading connective prints also; thus in the final entry the qualifier consists of a phrase. The downwards reading connective attached to 'Hen' is printed until 'Hen' passes into the qualifier position. See Sections 4.5 to 4.7.

10   CAT
          Dog. Hen. Pig
      DOG. Cat
          Hen. Pig
      HEN. Fly
          Pig
      PIG. Hen. Fly

'Fly' is a substitute term which is to replace the specified number of higher terms (ie terms above it in the string) whenever any lower term (ie any term below it in the string) is in the lead. The specified number of terms in this case is two—(Sub 2). Thus when 'Hen' appears in the lead 'Fly' replaces 'Dog' and 'Cat' in the qualifier. See Section 4.4.

Checking exercise 2
Answers
(NB: The various notes (eg *Note 1*) refer to remedial notes which will
be found at the end of the model answers for this exercise. These should
be referred to if your answer does not agree with the model answer.

1   UNITED STATES
        Agricultural tractors. Tariffs
        Note 1
     TRACTORS. United States
        Agricultural tractors. Tariffs
        Notes 1, 2
     AGRICULTURAL TRACTORS. United States
        Tariffs
        Note 3
     TARIFFS. Agricultural tractors. United States
        Note 1

2   UNITED STATES
        Battery powered electric vehicles. Testing
        Note 1
     VEHICLES. United States
        Battery powered electric vehicles. Testing
        Notes 1, 2
     ELECTRIC VEHICLES. United States
        Battery powered electric vehicles. Testing
        Notes 1, 2
     BATTERY POWERED ELECTRIC VEHICLES. United States
        Testing
        Notes 3, 4
     TESTING. Battery powered electric vehicles. United States
        Note 1

3   WESTERN AUSTRALIA
        Gold. Mining, *1893-1973*
        Note 5
     GOLD. Western Australia
        Mining, *1893-1973*
     MINING. Gold. Western Australia
        1893-1973
        Note 6

123

4   CZECHOSLOVAKIA
    Reinforced cylindrical steel shells. Manufacture
    Note 1
SHELLS. Czechoslovakia
    Reinforced cylindrical stell shells. Manufacture
    Notes 1, 2
STEEL SHELLS. Czechoslovakia
    Reinforced cylindrical steel shells. Manufacture
CYLINDRICAL . . .
NB: No entry under 'cylindrical' because this term is coded $h,
ie *non-lead* direct difference.
REINFORCED SHELLS. Czechoslovakia
    Reinforced cylindrical steel shells. Manufacture
    Notes 1, 2, 7
No entry under 'Manufacture' because the term was not
ticked to appear in the lead.

5   GREAT BRITAIN
    Plastic insulated high-voltage electric cables. Manufacture
    Note 1
CABLES. Great Britain
    Plastic insulated high-voltage electric cables. Manufacture
    Notes 1, 2
ELECTRIC CABLES. Great Britain
    Plastic insulated high-voltage electric cables. Manufacture
    Notes 1, 2
No entry under 'High-voltage'
    Note 8
INSULATED CABLES. Great Britain
    Plastic insulated high-voltage electric cables. Manufacture
    Notes 1, 2, 9
PLASTIC INSULATED CABLES. Great Britain
    Plastic insulated high-voltage electric cables. Manufacture
    Notes 1, 2, 10

6   industry $i mining $m tin
'Mining' is a direct difference: it qualifies the focus, 'industry'.
'Tin' is an indirect difference: it qualifies the difference, 'mining'.
    AUSTRALIA.
      Tin mining industry

INDUSTRY. Australia
  Tin mining industry
MINING INDUSTRY. Australia
  Tin mining industry
TIN MINING INDUSTRY. Australia

7   batteries $i traction $i lead-acid
Both differences are direct: they each qualify 'batteries'.
  AUSTRALIA.
    Lead-acid traction batteries
  BATTERIES. Australia
    Lead-acid traction batteries
  TRACTION BATTERIES. Australia
    Lead-acid traction batteries
  LEAD-ACID BATTERIES. Australia
    Lead-acid traction batteries

8   trees $i fruit $i deciduous
'Fruit'is a direct difference: it qualifies 'trees'.
'Deciduous' is also a direct difference: it qualifies 'trees'.
  AUSTRALIA.
    Deciduous fruit trees
  TREES. Australia
    Deciduous fruit trees
  FRUIT TREES. Australia
    Deciduous fruit trees
  DECIDUOUS TREES. Australia
    Deciduous fruit trees

9   dresses $i party $i nylon $m brushed $i blue $m dark $i new
'Party', 'nylon', 'blue' and 'new' are each a qualifier on 'dresses'.
'Brushed' is a qualifier on 'nylon', and 'dark' is a qualifier on 'blue'.
  AUSTRALIA
    New dark blue brushed nylon party dresses
  DRESSES. Australia
    New dark blue brushed nylon party dresses
  PARTY DRESSES. Australia
    New dark blue brushed nylon party dresses
  NYLON DRESSES. Australia
    New dark blue brushed nylon party dresses
125

BRUSHED NYLON DRESSES. Australia
New dark blue brushed nylon party dresses
BLUE DRESSES. Australia
New dark blue brushed nylon party dresses
DARK BLUE DRESSES. Australia
New dark blue brushed nylon party dresses
NEW DRESSES. Australia
New dark blue brushed nylon party dresses

10   migrants $i counselling services for
AUSTRALIA
Counselling services for migrants
MIGRANTS. Australia
Counselling services for migrants
COUNSELLING SERVICES FOR MIGRANTS. Australia
See para. 11.

Notes NB: Paragraph references are in all cases to Unit 3.
Note 1 The elements of the compound (differenced) term are read from the string beginning with the right hand element.
ie   String   DiCmB
      Entry   BCD
      String   tractors $i agricultural
      Entry   agricultural tractors
See para. 2.
Note 2 Because only part of the compound term is in the lead the full term prints as the first part of the display. See para. 3.
Note 3 Because the full compound term is in the lead it no longer appears as the first part of the display. See para. 3.
Note 4 'Battery powered' is coded $m, ie it is an indirect difference. Thus when it appears as the entry word it is attached to the difference which it qualifies, ie 'electric'. See para. 7.
Note 5 $d causes the dates to be printed in italics, preceded by a comma. See paras. 9.2 and 9.3.
Note 6 The comma disappears because the dates are now the first part of the display. See paras. 9.2 and 9.3.
Note 7 'Reinforced' is coded $i, ie it is a direct difference. Thus when it appears as the entry word it is linked directly to the focus. See para. 5.
Note 8 'High voltage' is coded $k, ie it is a *non-lead* indirect difference.
Note 9 'Insulated' is coded $i, ie it is a direct difference. Thus when it appears as the entry word it is linked directly to the focus. See para. 5.
Note 10 'Plastic' is coded $m, ie it is an indirect difference. Thus when it appears as the entry word it is attached to the difference which it qualifies, ie 'insulated'. See para. 7.

Checking exercise 3
Answers

1   (0) Great Britain
    (1) cinema films $i silent
    (2) distribution $d c.1920-1929
Cinema films is treated as a single term, as the example in Unit 3
demonstrated (see Unit 2, 10.3).

The action is distribution, and the object of the action (the key
system) is cinema films. This is differenced: *silent* cinema films. The
location is Great Britain.

The date is placed as low in the string as possible without disturbing
the meaning.

2   (1) dogs
    (2) digestion $v of $w by
    (3) meat $h raw
The action is digestion and is coded (2). Because the action is a physiological process the object is coded (3) and the agent (1). See para. 6.2.

It is questionable whether or not an entry is required under 'raw'. It
is coded here as a non-lead difference ($h); however it could validly be
coded $i if it is thought that an entry is required under this term.

3   (0) London
    (1) roads
    (2) congestion $v by $w of
    (3) road traffic
If the subject is analyzed carefully it will be seen that we have an action
(congestion) which has an object (roads) and an agent: traffic (or, more
accurately, road traffic—to distinguish from, for example, air traffic).

4   (0) France
    (1) radicalism
    (3) social aspects
In this case we have no action term. However, we have an abstract
thing (radicalism) and a term denoting an aspect of it. The aspect term
is coded (3) and radicalism is coded (1). France, as the location, is
coded (0).

5   (0) Victoria
    (1) clothing industries
    (2) economic conditions

Economic conditions belongs to the category of 'phenomena' and should be coded (2)—see para. 4.3 of this unit. Clothing industries is not entered as a differenced term (industries $i clothing) because if all industries were entered in this way an excessive number of entries would be generated under 'industries'. Instead a reference would be generated:

INDUSTRIES
　　See also
　　CLOTHING INDUSTRIES

6　(1)　boats $i sailing $h small　　←——— Object
　　(2)　hiring　　　　　　　　　　←——— Transitive action

Small could be coded $i if it is thought that an entry is required under this term.

7　(1)　children $i handicapped $m physically
　　(2)　education $w of
　　(2)　administration

Here we have two actions. For a discussion of the order see para. 4.4 of this unit. 'Physically handicapped children' is the object of the first action. The upwards reading connective could possibly be omitted.

8　(1)　children
　　(2)　mental development $w of
　　(2)　measurement

9　(1)　investment funds
　　(2)　misappropriation $w of
　　(2)　investigation $v by $w of
　　(3)　accountants

Here we have two actions with the object of the first action and the agent of the second.

10　(1)　water
　　(2)　conservation

11　BUILDINGS
　　Damage by frost
　　DAMAGE. Buildings
　　By frost

128

FROST
   Damage to buildings
Note the predicate transformation in the third entry, see paras. 7.1 to
7.3 of this unit.

12   NEW YORK
        Greek migrants. Education
     MIGRANTS. New York
        Greek migrants. Education
     GREEK MIGRANTS. New York
        Education
     EDUCATION. Greek migrants. New York

13   FRUIT TREES
        Contamination by toxic insecticides
     CONTAMINATION. Fruit trees
        By toxic insecticides
     INSECTICIDES
        Toxic insecticides. Contamination of fruit trees
     TOXIC INSECTICIDES
        Contamination of fruit trees
Note the predicate transformation in the two final entries. Note also
that the differenced term is manipulated *before* predicate transformation occurs (see para 7.5 of this unit).

14   EUROPE
        Long pre-stressed concrete bridges. Construction
     BRIDGES. Europe
        Long pre-stressed concrete bridges. Construction
     CONCRETE BRIDGES. Europe
        Long pre-stressed concrete bridges. Construction
     PRE-STRESSED CONCRETE BRIDGES. Europe
        Long pre-stressed concrete bridges. Construction
     CONSTRUCTION. Long pre-stressed concrete bridges. Europe

15   VICTORIA
        Livestock. Destruction by bushfires, *1977*
     LIVESTOCK. Victoria
        Destruction by bushfires, *1977*
     DESTRUCTION. Livestock. Victoria
        By bushfires, *1977*
     BUSHFIRES. Victoria
        1977. Destruction of livestock
                        129

Checking exercise 4
Answers

1   (1) cattle
    (p) musculoskeletal systems
    (p) anatomy
There is no action term. The subject is anatomy which is a property of
musculoskeletal systems which in turn are a part of cattle (para. 1 of
Unit 4).

2   (1) aborigines
    (p) sacred objects
    (2) conservation
Conservation is an action. The entities being conserved are sacred
objects which are a property of aborigines, thus 'aborigines' is coded (1)
and 'sacred objects' (p).

3   (0) Scotland
    (1) collies $i rough
    (2) breeding
Breeding is an action and coded (2) and the object of the action is
'rough collies'. Scotland is the location. It is incorrect to code 'rough
collies' as (q) with 'dogs' (1) since rough collies are, by definition, dogs,
ie this is a true generic relationship and would be covered by a reference:
    DOGS
        See also
        COLLIES

4   (0) Bohemia
    (1) glassware
    (q) bowls $i glass $i decorative
    (2) manufacture
Manufacture is an action and the entities being manufactured are bowls.
'Bowls' is a homonym (game or glassware), therefore 'glassware' is
included in the string, with 'bowls' being (q). The difference 'decorative' is attached to bowls; the document is concerned with decorative
bowls, glassware being included in the string only because 'bowls' is a
homonym. Note that glassware is not ticked to appear in the lead
because all decorative glass bowls are glassware (see para. 3.6.2 of Unit
4).

130

5   (1)   aircraft $i supersonic
     (q)   Concorde
     (p)   noise
     (2)   measurement
'Measurement' could possibly be ticked to appear as a lead.

6   (1)   sheep
     (r)   flocks
(sub 2)(1) sheep flocks
     (2)   herding $v by $w of
     (3)   kelpies
Note the substitute phrase (see para. 2.3.1 of Unit 4).

7   (0)   France
     (1)   cathedrals (NU)
     (q)   Chartres Cathedral
     (p)   windows
     (p)   stained glass
Chartres Cathedral is a 'class-of-one', thus it is coded (q) and cathedrals
is included in the string as the class of things to which it belongs. Note
the 'c' accompanying the tick for the 'class-of-one'. (See para. 3.6.3 of
this unit). Cathedrals is marked (NU) as it is not required in the qualifier position, ie there is no point in printing 'cathedrals' after 'Chartres
Cathedral'.

8   (1)   primary schools
     (p)   curriculum subjects
     (q)   science
Because 'curriculum subjects' has to be included in the string to explain
'woodwork' it is included for all subjects (see para. 3.6.1 of this unit).

9   (0)   Australia
     (1)   colleges of advanced education
     (p)   students
     (p)   academic achievement
NB: Australia should be coded (0), *not*:
     (1)   colleges of advanced education $i Australian
(See para. 10 of Unit 2).

10   (1)   tools $i cutting $i Stone Age
     (p)   blades
     (2)   fashioning

131

11   BUILDING SITES
         Lifting equipment: Cranes. Safety
      CRANES. Lifting equipment. Building sites
         Safety
      SAFETY. Cranes. Lifting equipment. Building sites

12   OFFICES
         Digital computer systems: IBM system 360/40. Programming
      DIGITAL COMPUTER SYSTEMS. Offices
         IBM system 360/40. Programming
      IBM SYSTEM 360/40. Digital computer systems. Offices
         Programming
      PROGRAMMING. IBM system 360/40. Digital computer
                        systems. Offices

13   FISH
         Shoals. Detection by radar
      RADAR
         Detection of fish shoals

14   ADELAIDE
         Art festivals: Adelaide Festival, *1978*
      ART FESTIVALS. Adelaide
         Adelaide Festival, *1978*
      ADELAIDE FESTIVAL
         1978

15   VEGETABLES
         Contamination by insecticides: Organochlorine compounds
      CONTAMINATION. Vegetables
         By insecticides: Organochlorine compounds
      INSECTICIDES
         Organochlorine compounds. Contamination of vegetables
      ORGANOCHLORINE COMPOUNDS. Insecticides
         Contamination of vegetables

132

Checking exercise 5
Answers

1   (1) aćademic libraries
    (p) uşers (NU)
    (q) sťudents
    (3) stock
    (q) périodicals
(sub 3)(p) periodicals to students
    (2) lóan
    (6) regulations

2   (2) mílitary life
    (4) sóciological perspectives
If you made mistakes in your string re-work paragraph 1.1 of Unit 5.

3   (0) Aŭstralia
    (1) cárs
    (p) spáre parts
    (p) príces
    (6) inquiry reports
Inquiry reports should not be ticked to appear in the lead. It is in the highest degree unlikely that a user would seek for this subject in the index by looking under that term, nor is it likely that one would wish to retrieve all inquiry reports (by conducting a search on that term). In general a term coded (6) as form of presentation should only be ticked as a lead if it denotes or implies an activity, and if it would not generate an excessive number of entries. Thus *walkers' guides* would be ticked but not *travel guides*.

4   (0) Nëw South Wales
    (1) médical services (NU)
    (q) Róýal Flying Doctor Service
Note that the Royal Flying Doctor Service is a 'class-of-one' (see para. 3.6.3 of Unit 4).

5   (2) státistics
    (6) sócial sciences $h for

6   (1) pípes $i water $m hot $i insulated $m thermally
    (2) manufacture
If you made errors in the string re-work paras. 2-7 of Unit 2.

133

7 (2) anatomy
   (6) nursing $h for

8 (0) London
   (1) libraries
   (p) stock
   (q) periodicals
   (6) union lists

Note that 'stock' is inserted into the string to explain 'periodicals', see 3.6.1 of Unit 4. Otherwise the entry under periodicals will be ambiguous.

   PERIODICALS. Libraries. London
        — *Union lists*

ie periodicals *in*, or periodicals *about*, libraries.

9 It is necessary to analyse, and encode in the string, all the concepts embodied in the term 'Medibank':
   (0) Australia
   (1) health services
   (q) Medibank
   (4) trade union viewpoints

If 'Health services' is coded NU then the term would not appear in the entry under MEDIBANK.

10 (0) Australia
    (1) social welfare
    (p) statistics
    (6) conference proceedings
    (6) bibliographies

Note that statistics is coded (p) as a software component, whereas in earlier examples it was coded (2) because what was involved there was the discipline of statistics, not actual sets of statistics.

11 CALIFORNIA
        Goldfields. Social conditions, *1852 — Personal observations*
    GOLDFIELDS. California
        Social conditions, *1852 — Personal observations*
    SOCIAL CONDITIONS. Goldfields. California
        1852 — Personal observations

134

12 PHYSICS
    – *Secondary school texts* – *Bibliographies*

13 NEW ZEALAND
    Unemployment. Government policies – *Sociological perspectives*
    UNEMPLOYMENT. New Zealand
    Government policies – *Sociological perspectives*
    GOVERNMENT POLICIES. Unemployment. New Zealand
    – *Sociological perspectives*
    SOCIOLOGICAL PERSPECTIVES
    New Zealand. Unemployment. Government policies

14 NORTHERN TERRITORY
    Aborigines. Land rights – *Mining company viewpoints*
    ABORIGINES. Northern Territory
    Land rights – *Mining company viewpoints*
    LAND RIGHTS. Aborigines. Northern Territory
    – *Mining company viewpoints*
    MINING COMPANY VIEWPOINTS
    Northern Territory. Aborigines. Land rights

15 GREAT BRITAIN
    Sport – *Conference proceedings*
    SPORT. Great Britain
    – *Conference proceedings*

Checking exercise 6
Answers
(In the answers below, a country is always marked to appear as a lead when coded (0). Students should note,. however, that their own country, when coded (0), should not appear as a lead. Thus British students should *not* tick 'Great Britain' in question 8 nor Australian students 'Australia' in question 5.)

1   (0) China
     (p) coastal waters
     (1) shipwrecks
If you coded 'China' (1) refer to para. 3.1.1 of Unit 6.

2   (0) Melbourne
     (1) migrants $i Greek
     (p) living standards
     (5) study regions
     (q) Fitzroy
The form 'living standards' is preferred to 'standards of living' because this brings the more significant word to the front. If your string was not correct in the coding of 'Fitzroy' see para. 3.1 of Unit 6.

3   (1) postage stamps $i New Zealand
     (6) catalogues
Postage stamps are exportable, hence New Zealand is coded as a difference (Unit 2, para. 10).

4   (1) Great Britain
     (2) social conditions $d c.1801-1900
See paras. 4.1 and 4.2 of Unit 6.

5   (0) Australia
     (1) cars
     (p) spare parts
     (p) prices
     (6) inquiry reports

6   (1) paintings $i water-colour $i English $d c.1801-1900
     (6) catalogues
'English' is coded as a difference because 'paintings' is an exportable concept. See para. 10 of Unit 2.

7   (1) Great Britain
    (p) coastal waters
    (6) charts

8   (0) Great Britain
    (1) canals (NU)
    (q) Grand Union Canal
    (6) guidebooks
'Great Britain' is coded (0) because canals represents an entity whose
name implies an actual or intended use by man.

9   (1) Greece
    (p) rural areas
    (2) social life
See paras. 4.1 and 4.2 of Unit 6.

10 (0) Wales
    (1) onions
    (2) sales $v by $w of
    (3) France $i salesmen from $m itinerant
This string is more accurate than
    (0) Wales
    (1) onions
    (2) sales $v by $w of
    (3) salesmen $i French $i itinerant

11 CZECHOSLOVAKIA
       Prague — *Travel guides*
    PRAGUE. Czechoslovakia
       — *Travel guides*

12 IRELAND
       Rural areas. Social conditions
    RURAL AREAS. Ireland
       Social conditions
    SOCIAL CONDITIONS. Rural areas. Ireland

13 MELBOURNE
       Hospitals for children: Royal Children's Hospital
    CHILDREN. Melbourne
       Hospitals for children: Royal Children's Hospital

HOSPITALS FOR CHILDREN. Melbourne
Royal Children's Hospital
ROYAL CHILDREN'S HOSPITAL. Melbourne

14   GREAT BRITAIN
Climate, *c.1801-1900*
CLIMATE. Great Britain
c.1801-1900

15   SYDNEY
Population: Aborigines. Economic conditions — *Study regions: Redfern*
POPULATION. Sydney
Aborigines. Economic conditions — *Study regions: Redfern*
ABORIGINES. Population. Sydney
Economic conditions — *Study regions: Redfern*
ECONOMIC CONDITIONS. Aborigines. Population. Sydney
— *Study regions: Redfern*
REDFERN. *Study regions*
Sydney. Population. Aborigines. Economic conditions

Checking exercise 7
Answers

1 (0) Lóndon
   (1) búildings
   (p) fóundations
   (2) eˇxcavation

2 (1) cárs
   (p) réliability $w of
   (s) effects $v of $w on
   (3) máss production
NB: Use of '$w of' after 'reliability' in order to bring down 'cars' into
the display when 'Mass production' is in the lead.

3 (1) eḿpiricism
   (t) compared with
   (1) rátionalism

4 (1) bús services
   (2) sˇcheduling $w of
   (s) application $v of $w in
   (3) qúeueing theory
NB: Use of '$w' to bring down 'bus services' into the display in the
final entry.

5 (1) méaning
   (t) $v expounded by $w expounding
   (3) ińformation theory

6 (1) hóusing
   (2) finance
(sub 2)(2) housing finance
   (s) role $v of $w in
   (3) bánks

7 (1) wíldlife
   (2) cónservation $w of
   (s) role $v of $w in
   (3) gáme reserves

139

8 (1) sṕace vehicles
   (2) control $w of
   (s) applications $v of $w in
   (3) cőmputers

9 (1) Gřeat Britain
   (2) hístory
(sub 2)(2) British history
   (t) $v expounded in $w expounding
   (1) fíction in English

10 (0) Uńited States
    (1) hígh schools
    (p) students
    (p) aćademic achievement
    (t) related to
    (p) sőcial class

11 UNIVERSITIES
        Students. Academic achievement. Attitudes of academic
            personnel
    STUDENTS. Universities
        Academic achievement. Attitudes of academic personnel
    ACADEMIC ACHIEVEMENT. Students. Universities
        Attitudes of academic personnel
    ACADEMIC PERSONNEL. Universities
        Attitudes to academic achievement of students

12 JUVENILES
        Crime *expounded by* sociology
    CRIME. Juveniles
        expounded by sociology
    SOCIOLOGY
        expounding juvenile crime

13 INDUSTRY
        Use of digital computers
    DIGITAL COMPUTERS
        Use in industry

14 AUSTRALIAN RULES FOOTBALL
      Compared with Soccer
    SOCCER
      Compared with Australian Rules Football

15 CHINA
      Factory workers. Productivity. Effects of background music
    FACTORY WORKERS. China
      Productivity. Effects of background music
    PRODUCTIVITY. Factory workers. China
      Effects of background music
    MUSIC
      Background music. Effects on productivity of factory workers
        in China

Checking exercise 8
Answers

1   (1) Chile
    (2) frontier disputes $v with $w with
    (1) Peru

2   (1) libraries
    (2) cooperation $v with $w with
    (1) museums

3   (0) Italy
    (1) apples $v &
    (g) pears
    (2) storage

4   (1) libraries
    (p) stock
    (q) cinema films
    (g) slides $v &
    (g) filmstrips
    (2) cataloguing

5   (1) prices
    (t) related to
    (1) incomes

6   (z)(0) Italy
    (x)(1) apples
    (y)(2) harvesting
    (x)(1) pears
    (y)(2) storage

7   (0) Japan
    (1) profits $v &
    (g) wages
    (t) related to
    (1) inflation

8   (1) Pacific Region
    (2) colonisation $v by $w of
    (3) France

142

9 (0) Great Britain
   (1) films $i Australian $v &
   (g) television programmes $i Australian
   (2) sales

A more satisfactory set of entries may be produced from the following string:

   (0) Great Britain
   (1) films $i Australian $v &
   (g) television programmes
   (1) television programmes $i Australian (LO)
   (2) sales

10 (z) (0) Canada
    (x) (1) cars
    (y) (p) seat belts
    (y) (2) use
    (y) (t) related to reduction in road accident deaths
    (x) (2) road accidents
    (y) (2) deaths
    (y) (2) reduction
    (y) (2) related to use of seat belts in cars

11 CHILDREN
        Attitudes of old people
    OLD PEOPLE
        Attitudes to children

12 FRANCE
        Mental hospitals. Personnel: Nurses. Absenteeism & sickness
    MENTAL HOSPITALS. France
        Personnel: Nurses. Absenteeism & sickness
    PERSONNEL. Mental hospitals. France
        Nurses. Absenteeism & sickness
    NURSES. Mental hospitals. France
        Absenteeism & sickness
    ABSENTEEISM. Nurses. Mental hospitals. France
    SICKNESS. Nurses. Mental hospitals. France

13 TELEVISION INDUSTRY. Australia
        Film scripts. Writing

143

FILM SCRIPTS. Television industry. Australia
   Writing
WRITING. Film scripts. Television industry. Australia
TELEVISION INDUSTRY. Australia
   Advertising. Administration
ADVERTISING. Television industry. Australia
   Administration
ADMINISTRATION. Advertising. Television industry. Australia

14   NAVIGATIONAL AIDS
      Use by ships, submarines & aircraft
    SHIPS
      Use of navigational aids
    SUBMARINES
      Use of navigational aids
    AIRCRAFT
      Use of navigational aids

15   UNITED STATES
      Trade with China
    TRADE. United States
      With China
    TRADE. China
      With United States
    CHINA
      Trade with United States

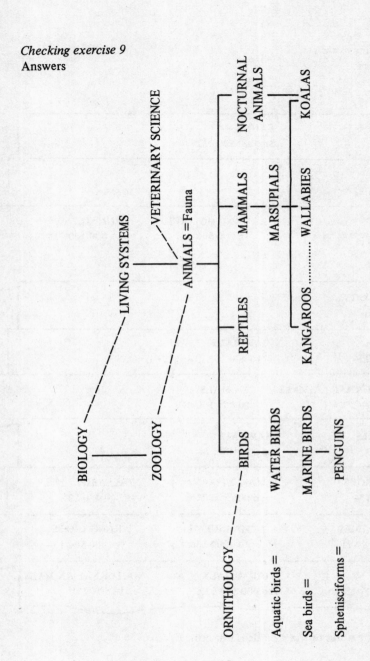

BIOLOGY

LIVING SYSTEMS

VETERINARY SCIENCE

ANIMALS = Fauna

ZOOLOGY

REPTILES

MAMMALS

MARSUPIALS

NOCTURNAL ANIMALS

KOALAS

KANGAROOS .... WALLABIES

BIRDS

WATER BIRDS

MARINE BIRDS

PENGUINS

ORNITHOLOGY

Aquatic birds =

Sea birds =

Sphenisciforms =

Checking exercise 10
Answers

1

ANIMALS   FAUNA
000 100 218 $m 000 600 022

FAUNA
000 600 022

BIRDS   ORNITHOLOGY   ANIMALS
000 400 254 $n 000 600 022 $o 000 100 218

ORNITHOLOGY
000 400 246

MAMMALS   ANIMALS
000 100 234 $o 000 100 218

NOCTURNAL ANIMALS   ANIMALS
018 509 231 $o 000 100 218

MARSUPIALS   MAMMALS
000 100 03X $o 000 100 234

KANGAROOS   MARSUPIALS   WALLABIES
000 500 134 $o 000 100 03X $x 000 478 121

WALLABIES   MARSUPIALS   KANGAROOS
000 478 121 $o   000 100 03X $x 000 500 134

KOALAS   MARSUPIALS   NOCTURNAL ANIMALS
000 682 031 $o 000 100 03X $o 018 509 231

NB: The order of the records is not critical.

2.1 IGNEOUS ROCKS
     See also
       GRANITE

ACIDIC ROCKS
  See also
    GRANITE

2.2 Laridae *See* GULLS

MARINE BIRDS
  See also
    GULLS

2.3 SOUTH ASIA
     See also
       SRI LANKA

Ceylon *See* SRI LANKA

2.4 ENERGY
     See also
       LIGHT

OPTICS
  See also
    LIGHT

2.5 AIR CONDITIONING
     See also
       VENTILATION

2.6 ETHNOLOGY
     See also
       SKULLS

Checking exercise 11
Answers

1   \$z01030\$aItaly\$z11030\$anatural resources\$zq1030\$arivers

2   \$z00030\$aAustralia\$z11030\$amigrants\$z21030\$aeducation

3   \$z11030\$avertebrates\$zp1030\$aanatomy\$z50030\$astudy examples
     \$zq1030\$adogfish

4   \$z01030\$aBohemia\$z11030\$aglassware\$zq1030\$abowls
     \$idecorative\$z20030\$amanufacture

5   \$z01030\$aVictoria\$z11030\$acables\$ielectrical\$khigh voltage
     \$iinsulated\$mplastic\$z20030\$amanufacture

6   \$z11030\$acrops\$z21030\$adamage\$vby\$wof\$z31030\$afrost

7   \$z11030\$aschools\$z21030\$aadministration\$zs0030\$arole\$vof
     \$win\$z31030\$ateachers

8   \$z11030\$ahippies\$zr1030\$acommunes\$z10220\$ahippie
     communes\$zp0030\$asocial structure

9   \$x11030\$aschools\$yp1010\$abuildings\$y21030\$aheat insulation
     \$x11030\$ahospitals\$yp1010\$abuildings\$yp1030\$awater supply
     services

10   \$z11030\$arural regions\$z21030\$aeconomic development\$wof
     \$zs0030\$arole\$vof\$win\$z31030\$asocial scientists\$z20420\$arole
     of social scientists in economic development of rural regions
     \$z21030\$aresearch

Checking exercise 12
Answers

1 (0) Europe
   (1) pipelines $i gas $m natural
   (2) design
Note: 'Design' could be ticked to appear as a lead if desired. Decisions such as this are at the discretion of the indexer and are not integral to the system.

2 (1) manuscripts $i illuminated $i Anglo-Saxon
   (2) preservation

3 (0) Australia
   (1) aborigines
   (p) land rights
   (6) inquiry reports
Note: Students in Australia should not have ticked 'Australia' to appear as a lead.

4 (0) Australia
   (1) controllers $i air traffic
   (2) strikes $d 1977
Note: The note for 3 above applies equally here. Also, a reference:
    TRAFFIC
        See also
            AIR TRAFFIC
is preferred to an entry under traffic:
   (1) controllers $i traffic $m air
because of the many entries likely to occur under traffic. It may also be debated whether 'traffic controllers' is likely to be a sought term.

5 (1) children
   (2) reading $w of
   (s) influence $v of $w on
   (3) television
Note: The use of the upwards reading connective to bring down 'children' in the final entry, ie
    TELEVISION
        Influence on reading of children
149

6 (0) Great Britain
   (1) secondary schools
   (p) curriculum subjects
   (q) typing

Note: Students in Britain should not tick 'Great Britain' to appear as a lead.

7 (0) France
   (1) war
   (s) attitudes $v of $w to
   (3) society

8 (0) London
   (1) airports
   (q) Heathrow Airport
   (p) runways
   (g) taxiways $g &
   (g) aviation aprons
   (2) extension

9 (0) London
   (1) art galleries
   (q) Wallace Collection
   (p) exhibits
   (q) paintings
   (6) catalogues

Note: The inclusion of 'exhibits' in the string to clarify the context of 'paintings'.

10 (1) mammals
    (p) endocrine system
    (2) secretion
    (3) hormones

Note: 'Secretion' is a physiological process, hence the agent is coded (1) and the object of the action (3).

11 MOTOR CAR INDUSTRY
        Advertising *related to* sales
     ADVERTISING. Motor car industry
        related to sales

150

SALES. Motor car industry
  related to advertising

12 VICTORIA
  Water birds — *Field guides*
  BIRDS. Victoria
  Water birds — *Field guides*
  WATER BIRDS. Victoria
  — *Field guides*

13 MELBOURNE
  Airports: Tullamarine Airport. Winds. Velocity.
    Measurement
  AIRPORTS. Melbourne
  Tullamarine Airport. Winds. Velocity. Measurement
  TULLAMARINE AIRPORT. Melbourne
  Winds. Velocity. Measurement
  WINDS. Tullamarine Airport. Melbourne
  Velocity. Measurement
  VELOCITY. Winds. Tullamarine Airport. Melbourne
  Measurement

14 TURTLES
  Ecology — *Study regions: Great Barrier Reef*
  ECOLOGY. Turtles
  — *Study regions: Great Barrier Reef*
  GREAT BARRIER REEF. *Study regions*
  Turtles. Ecology

15 NORTHERN TERRITORY
  Arnhem Land. Aboriginal rock carvings. Preservation
  ARNHEM LAND. Northern Territory
  Aboriginal rock carvings. Preservation
  ROCK CARVINGS. Arnhem Land. Northern Territory
  Aboriginal rock carvings. Preservation
  ABORIGINAL ROCK CARVINGS. Arnhem Land. Northern
        Territory
  Preservation
  PRESERVATION. Aboriginal rock carvings. Arnhem Land.
        Northern Territory

NORTHERN TERRITORY
   Arnhem Land. Aboriginal bark paintings. Collection
ARNHEM LAND. Northern Territory
   Aboriginal bark paintings. Collection
BARK PAINTINGS. Arnhem Land. Northern Territory
   Aboriginal bark paintings. Collection
ABORIGINAL BARK PAINTINGS. Arnhem Land. Northern
         Territory
   Collection